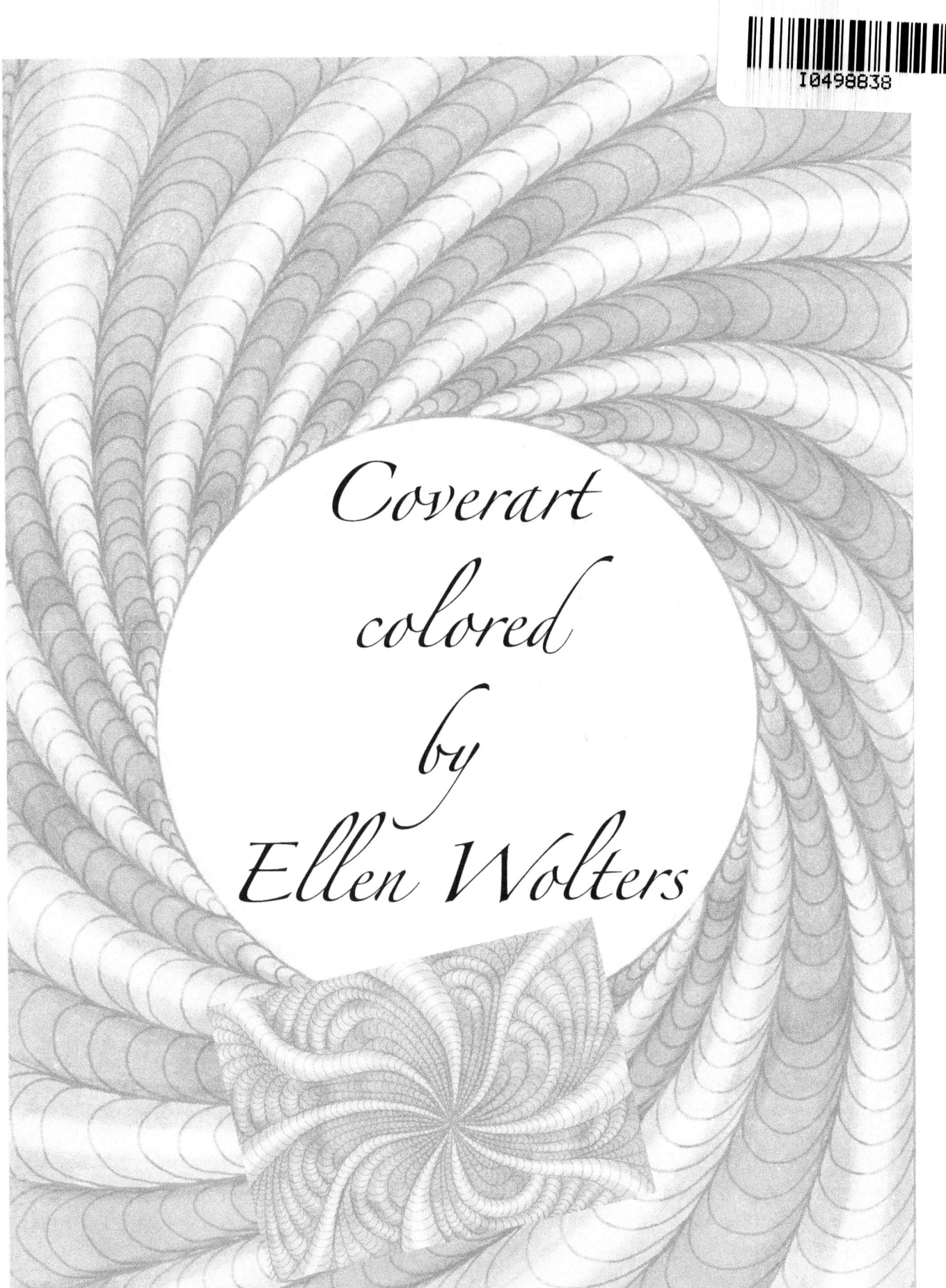

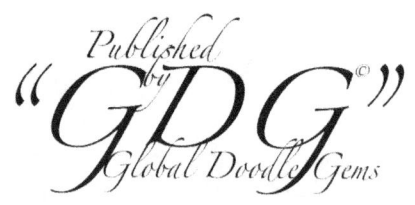

Share your colored versions with us ! We love seeing your results and hearing from you we are social !

The Official FB book page, stay on top of what we have in the works !
www.facebook.com/globaldoodlegems

The Community group, share your colored pages, meet the artists, enjoy exclusive freebies, take part in community Charity books and so much more......
www.facebook.com/groups/globaldoodlegems/

Follow us on Twitter.... @GlobalDoodlegem

We are on Instagram too
@globaldoodlegems for instagram

...and if you are not social like that we have a blog
globaldoodlegems.wordpress.com

Copyright © 2015 Global Doodle Gems

All rights are reserved by Global Doodle Gems.

Duplication of pages for personal use are allowed. You are invited to color the pages then scan/post your coloured versions to social networks, mentioning the book title and author/artist (Global Doodle Gems).

All artwork and images are protected by copyright laws. This book or any portion thereof may not, otherwise, be reproduced and/or distributed or transmitted without the express written permission of the artist/publisher of Global Doodle Gems.

All of us from the Global Doodle Gems wish you a colortastic time and look forward to seeing your wonderful color results online !

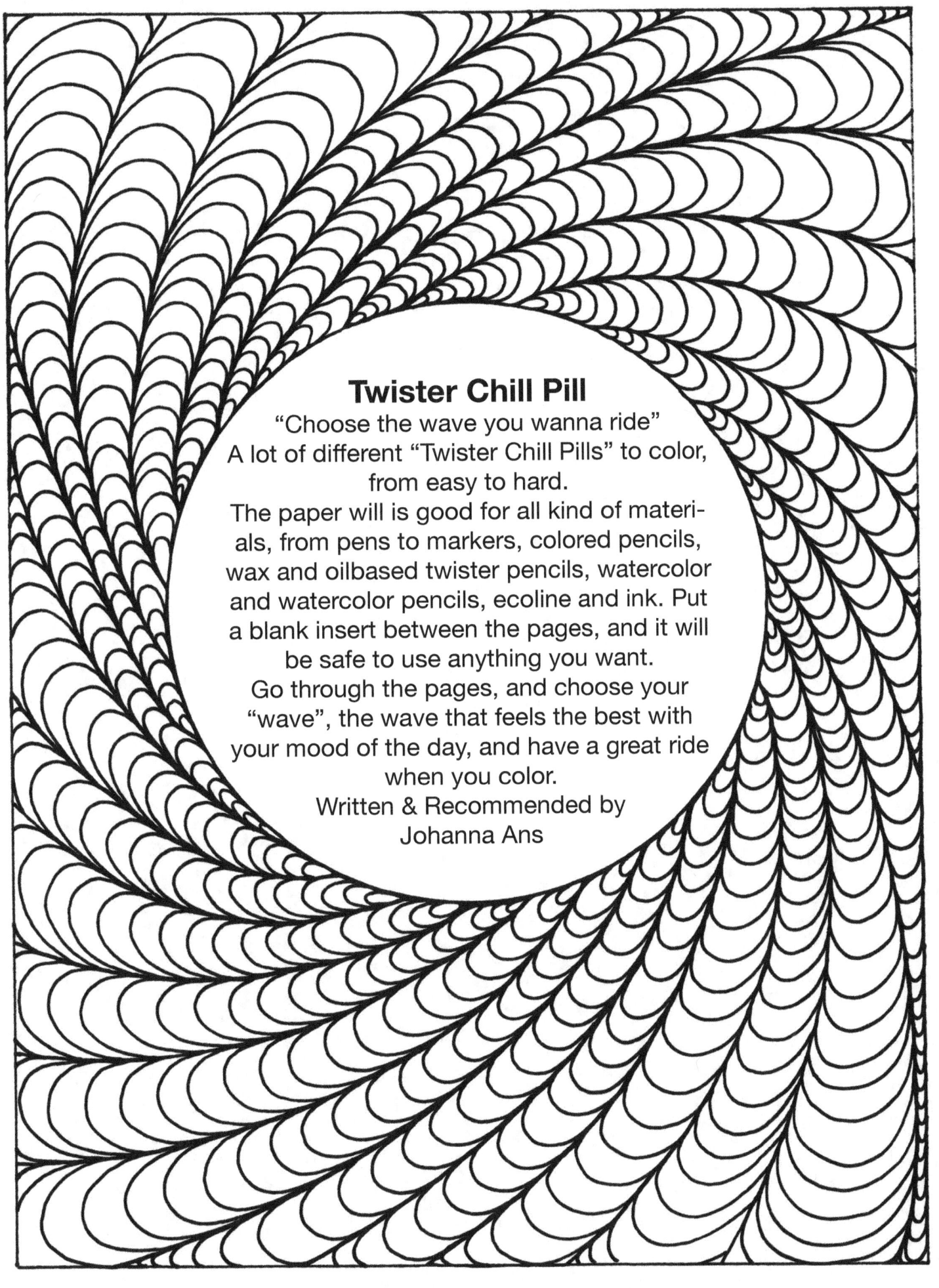

Twister Chill Pill

"Choose the wave you wanna ride"
A lot of different "Twister Chill Pills" to color, from easy to hard.
The paper will is good for all kind of materials, from pens to markers, colored pencils, wax and oilbased twister pencils, watercolor and watercolor pencils, ecoline and ink. Put a blank insert between the pages, and it will be safe to use anything you want.
Go through the pages, and choose your "wave", the wave that feels the best with your mood of the day, and have a great ride when you color.
Written & Recommended by
Johanna Ans

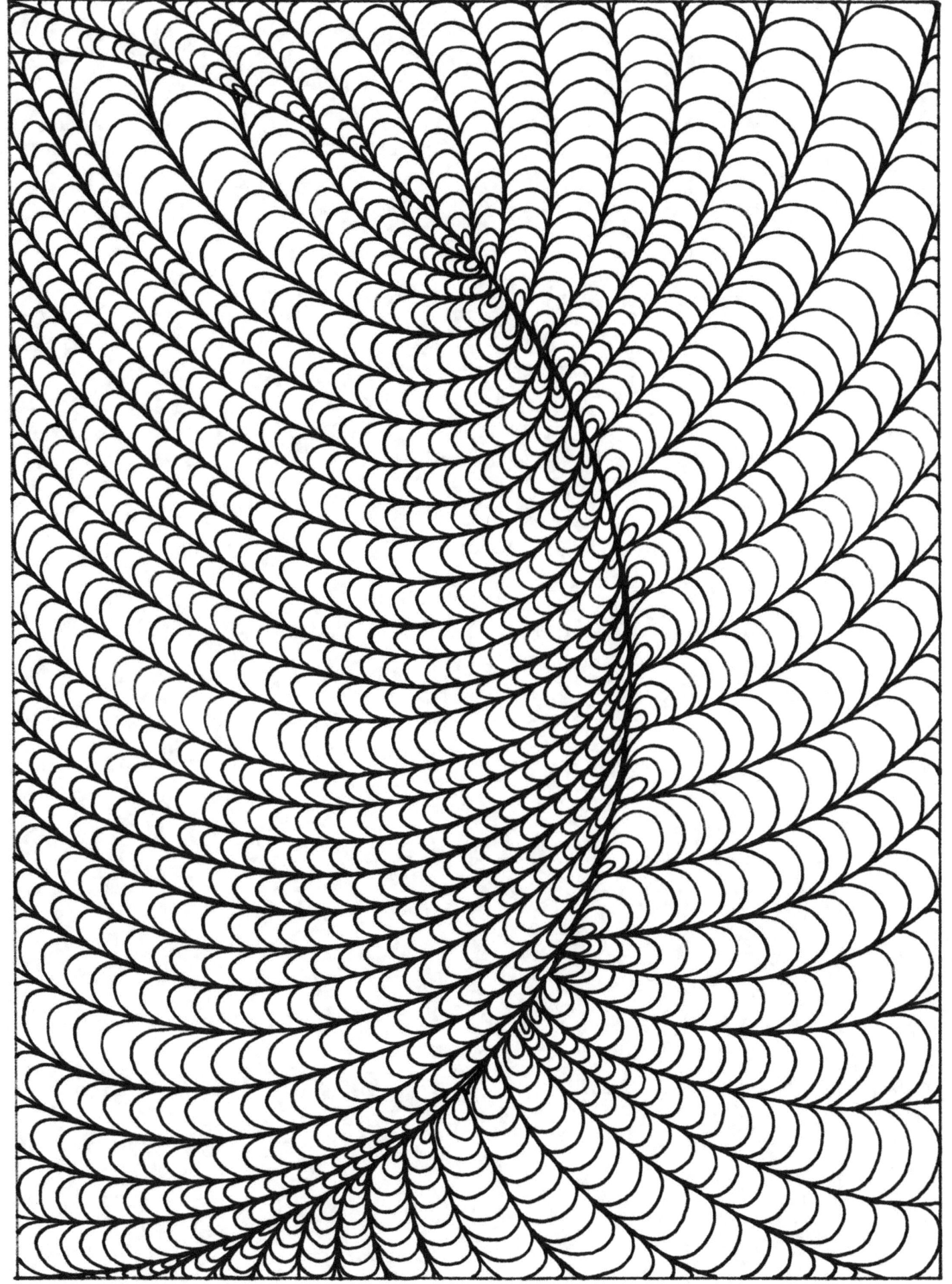

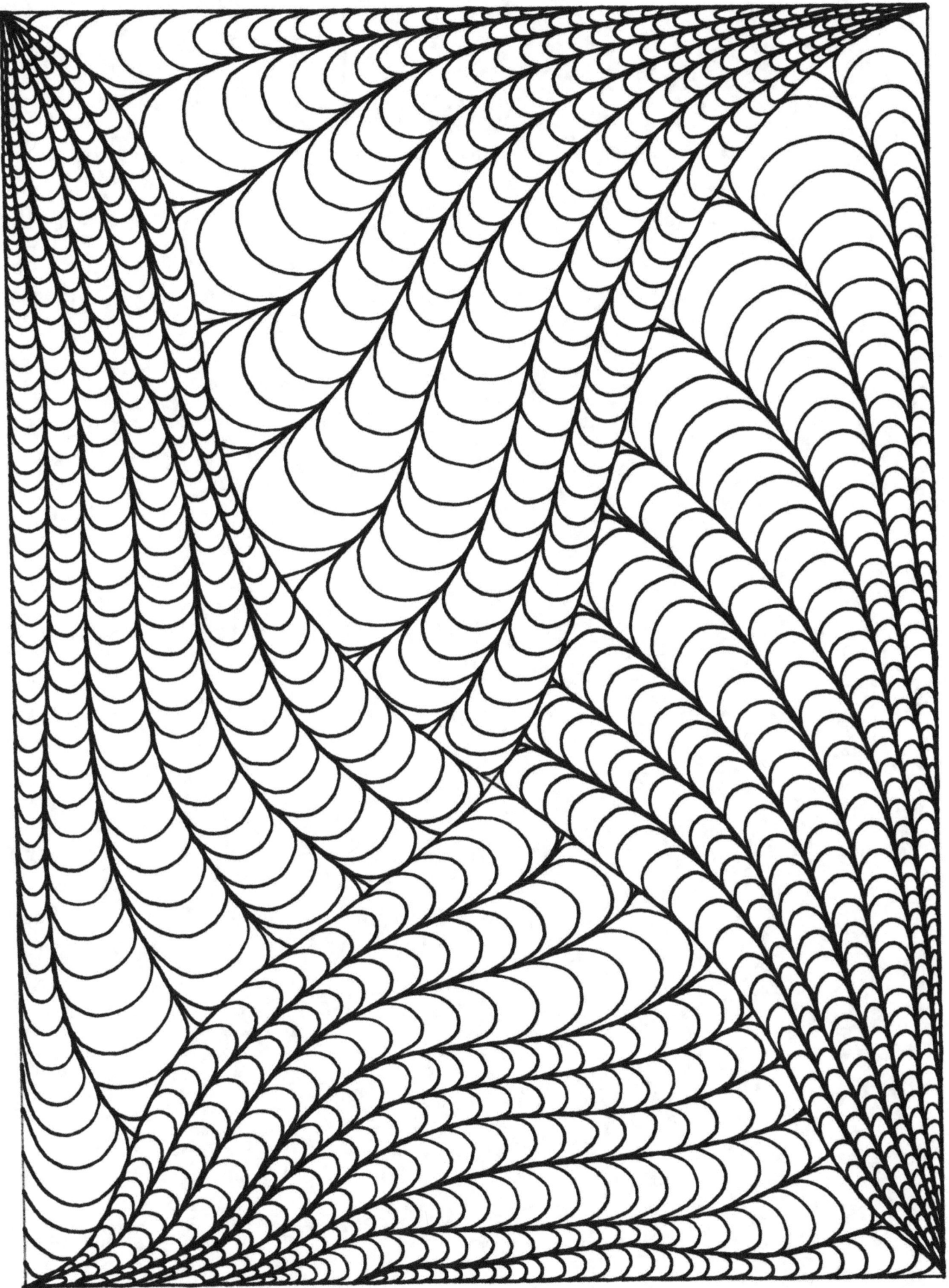

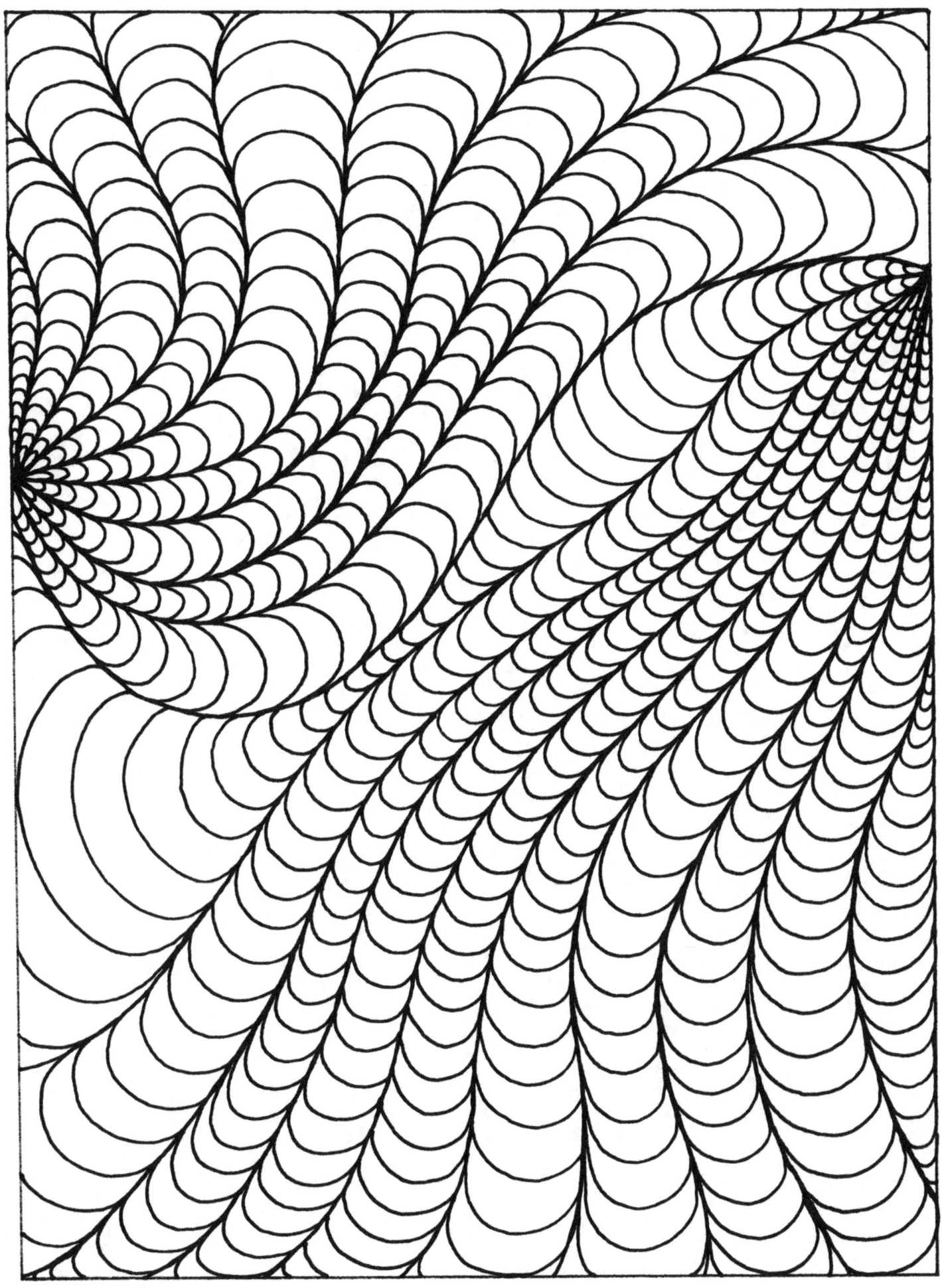

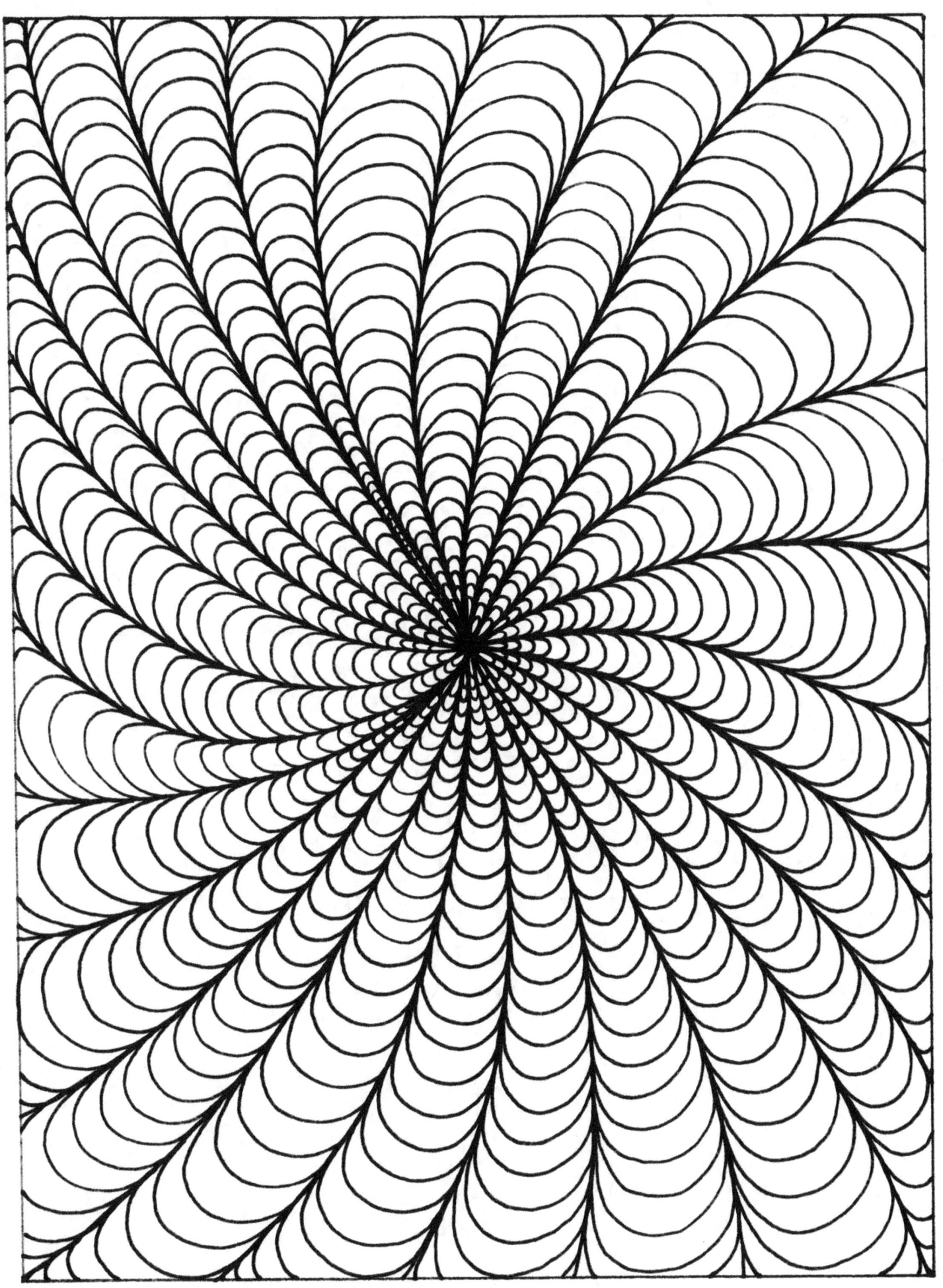

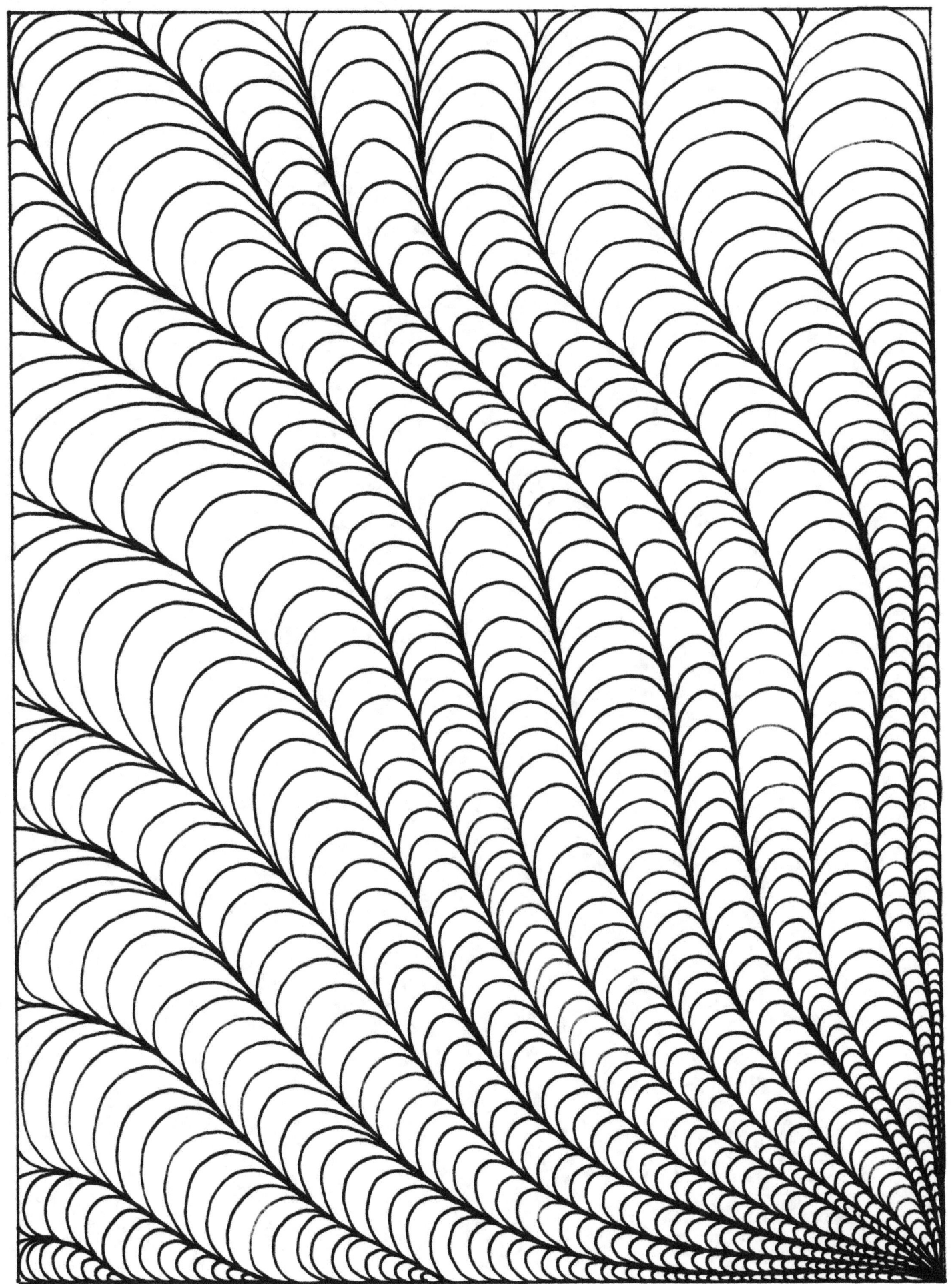

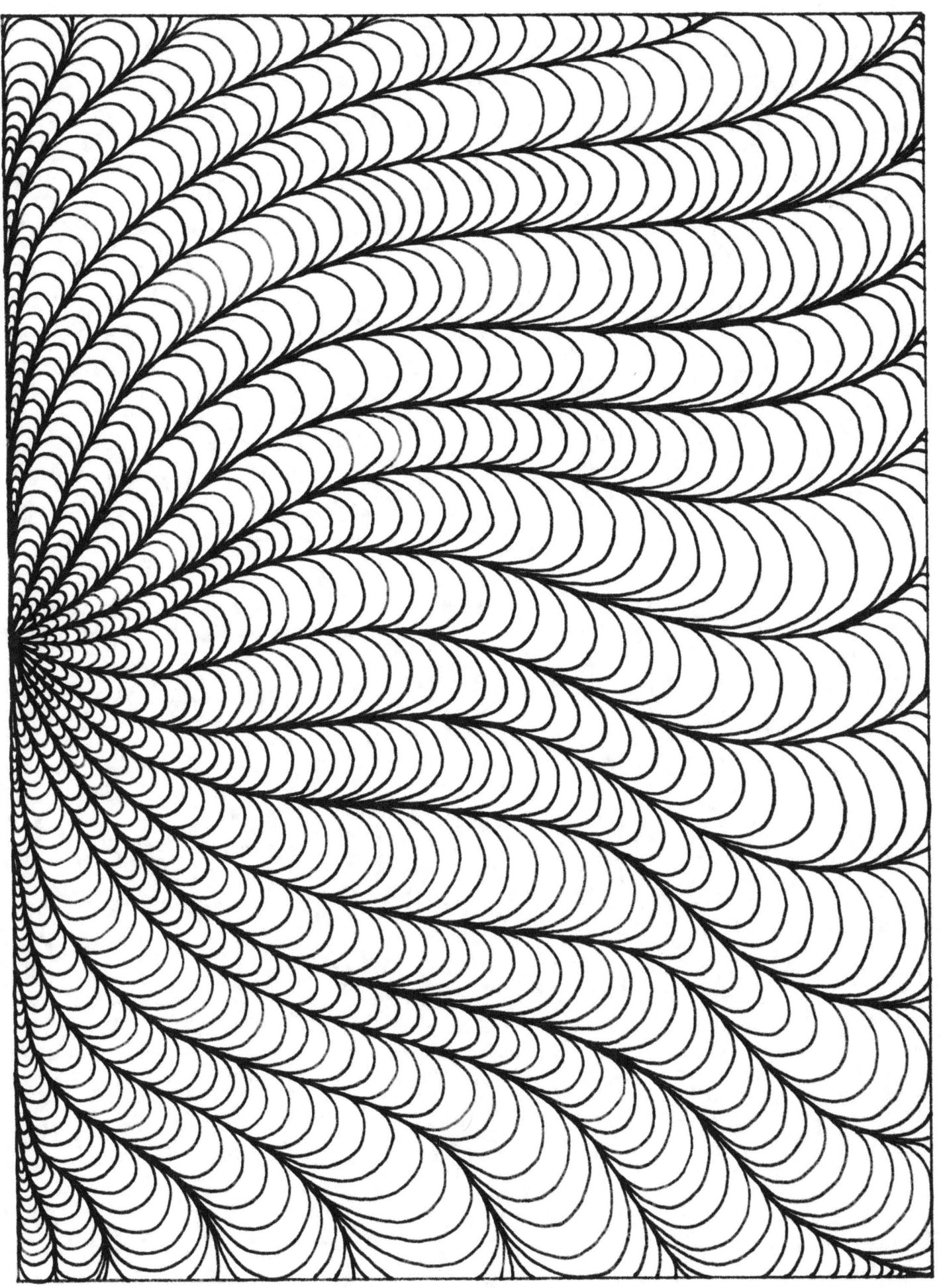

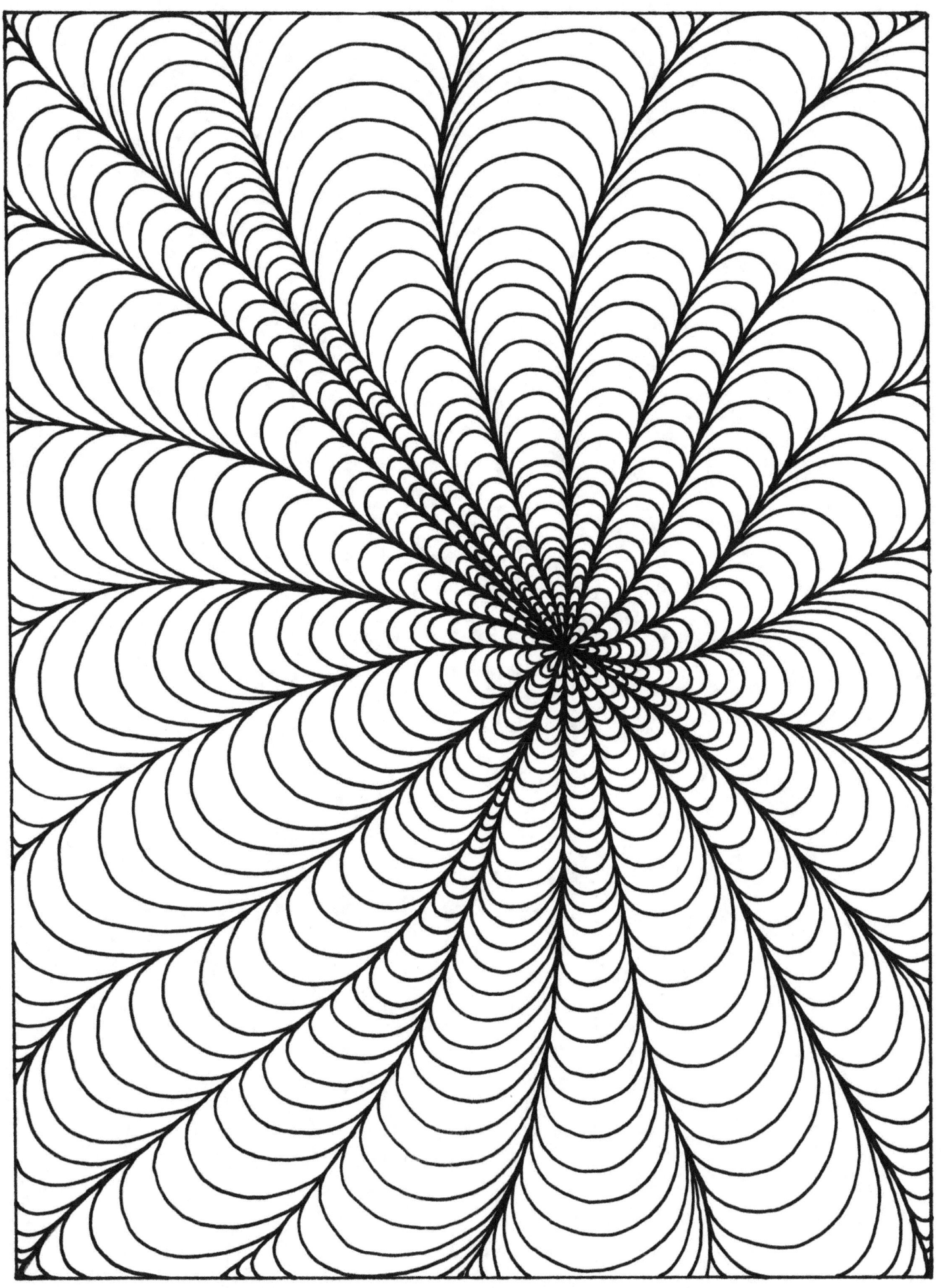

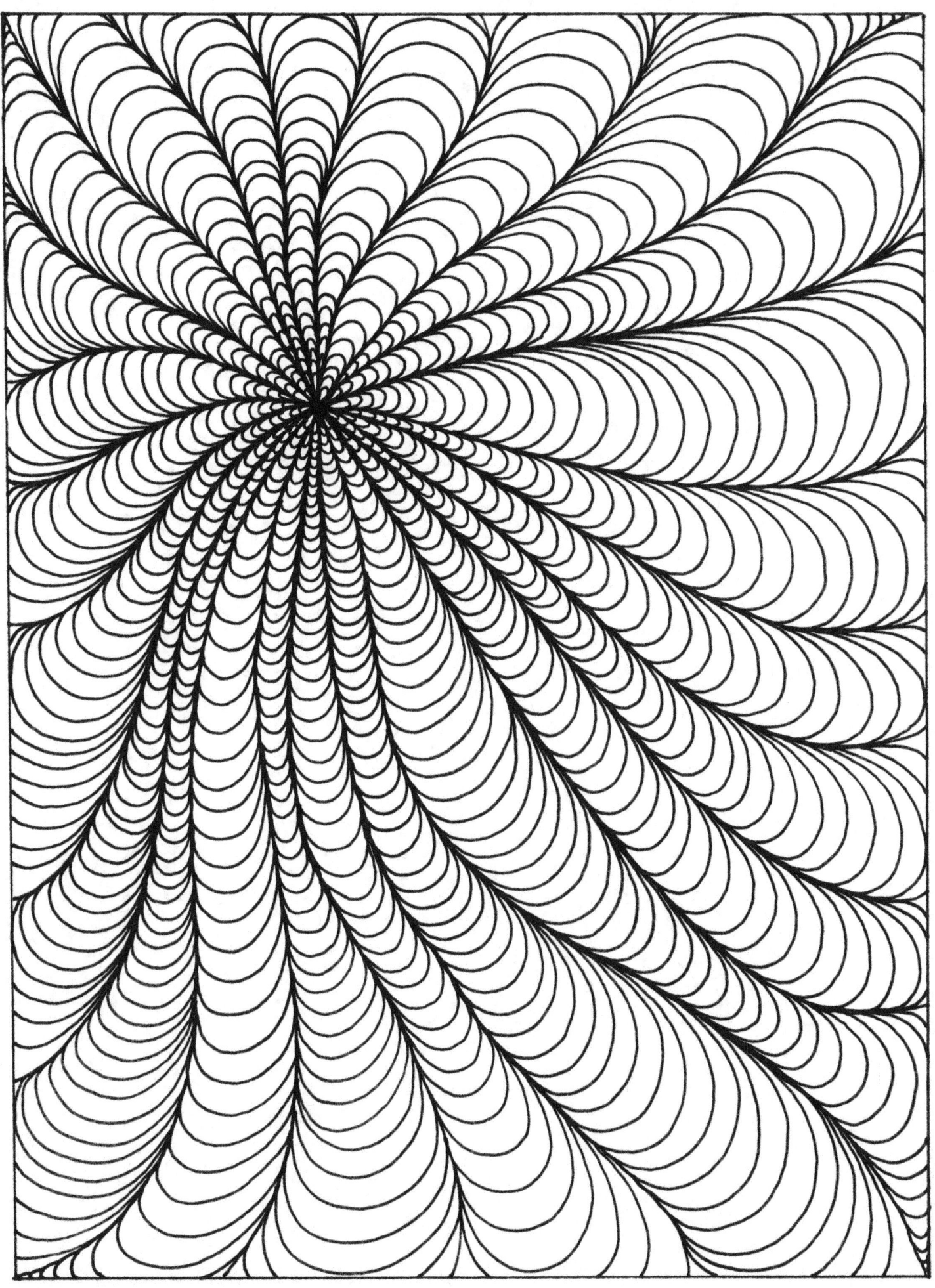

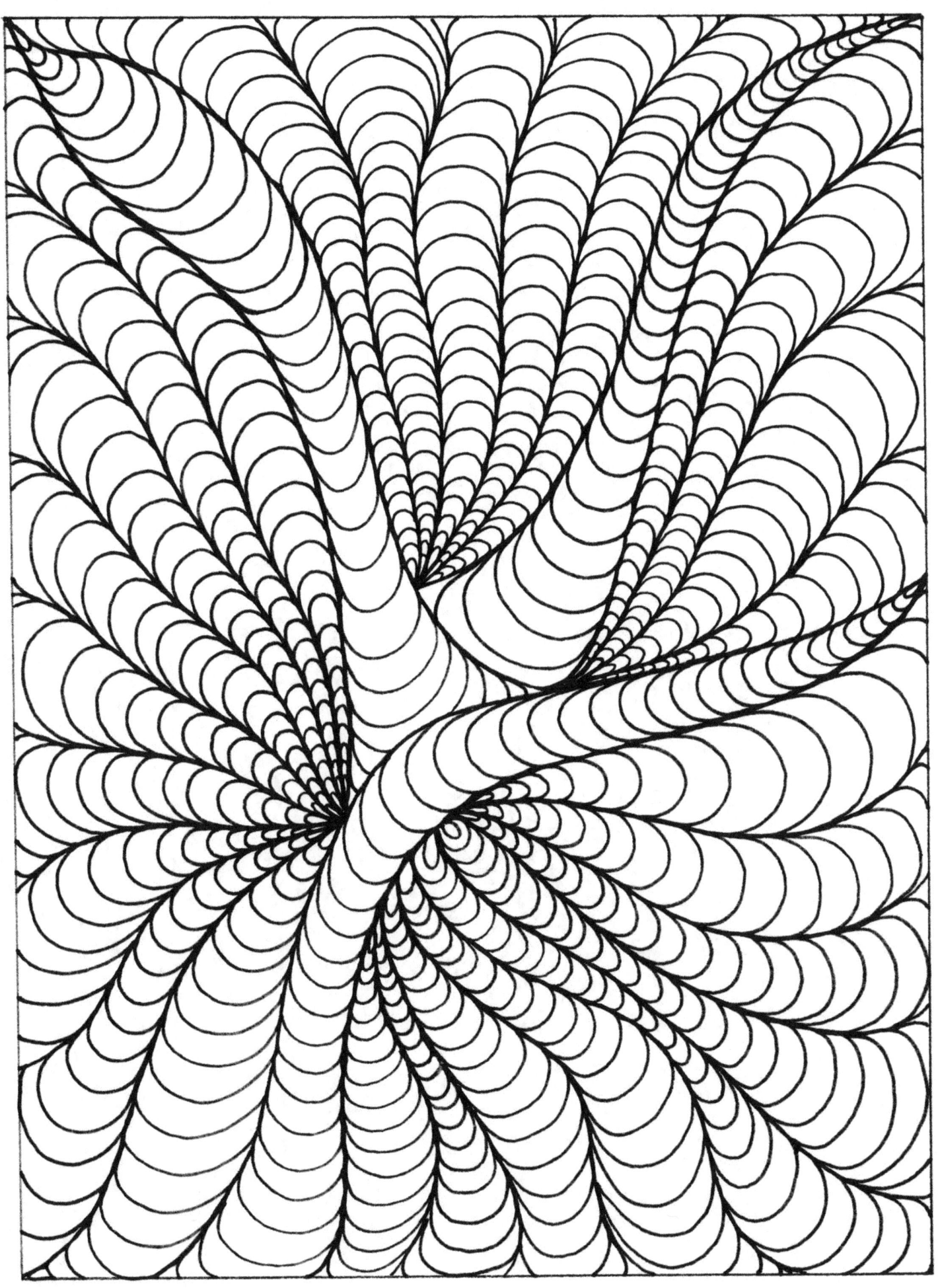

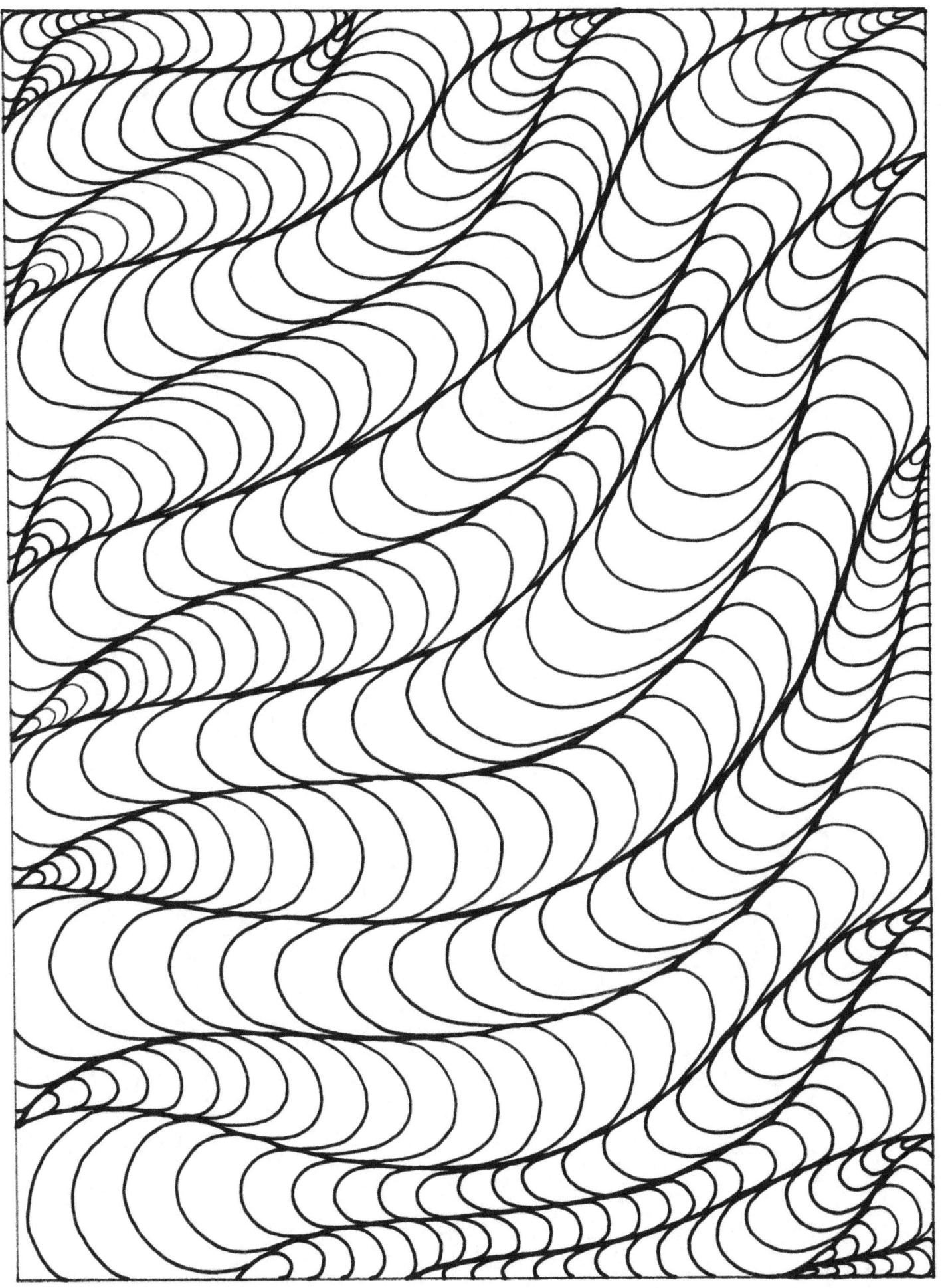

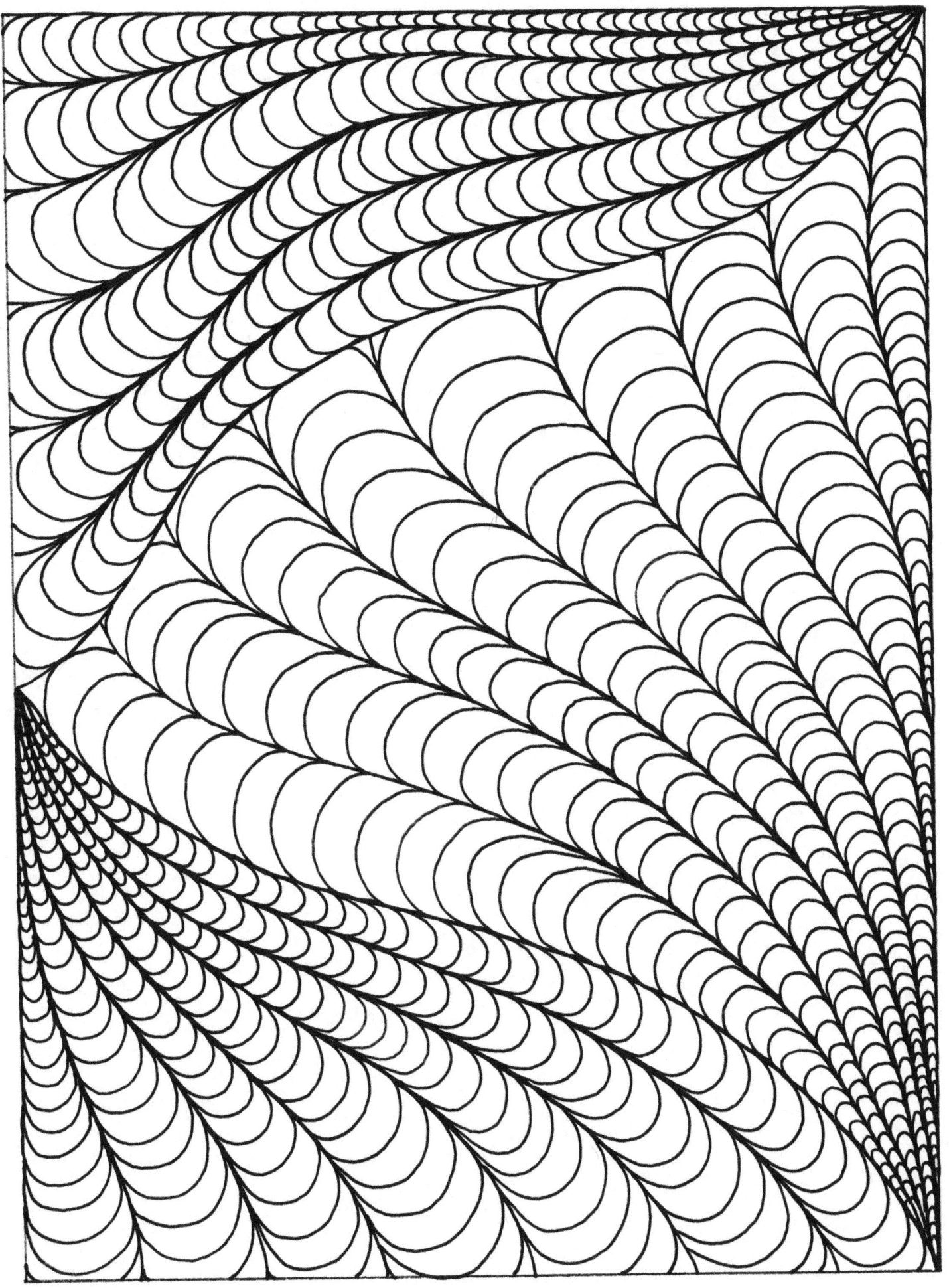

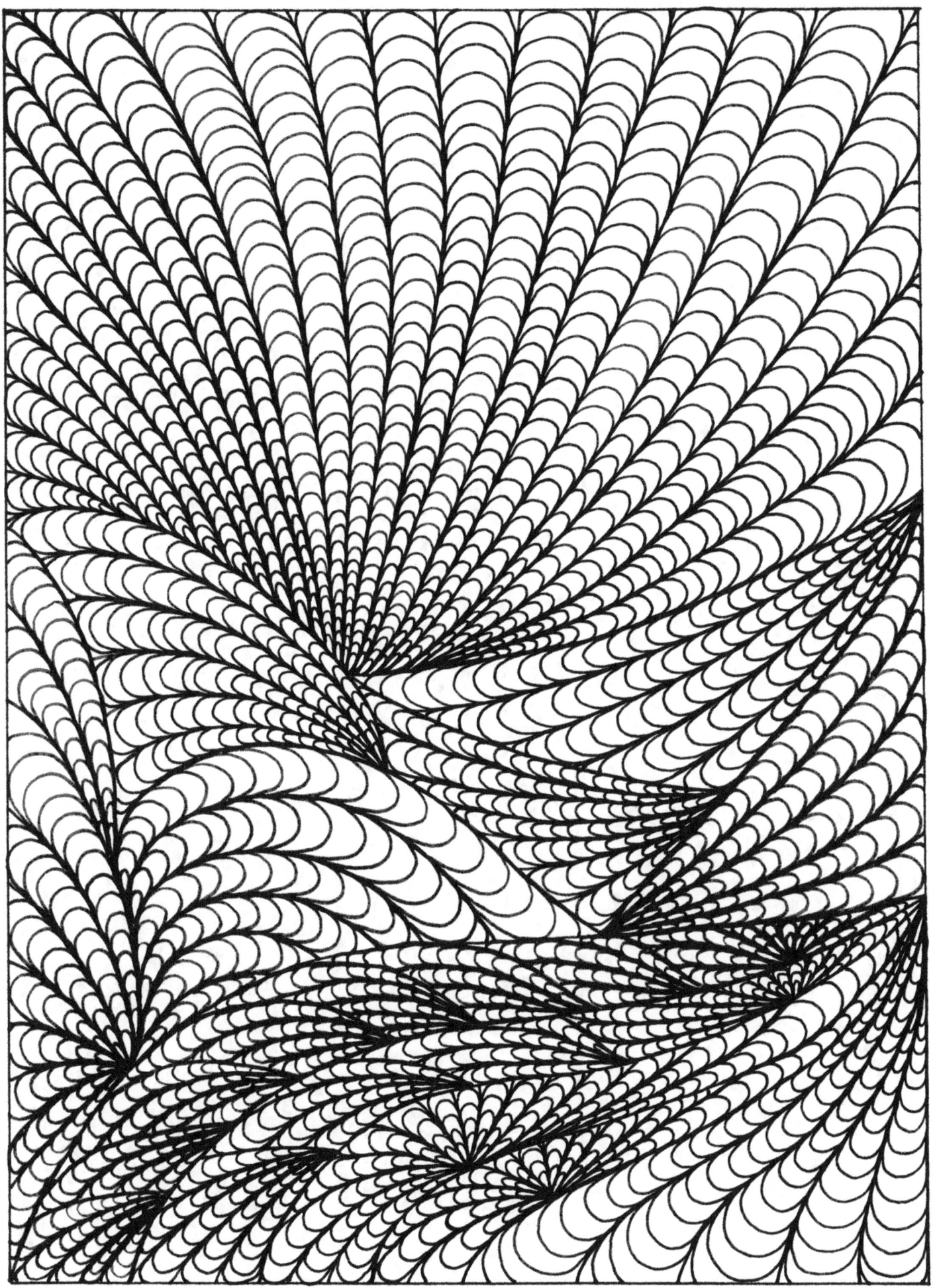

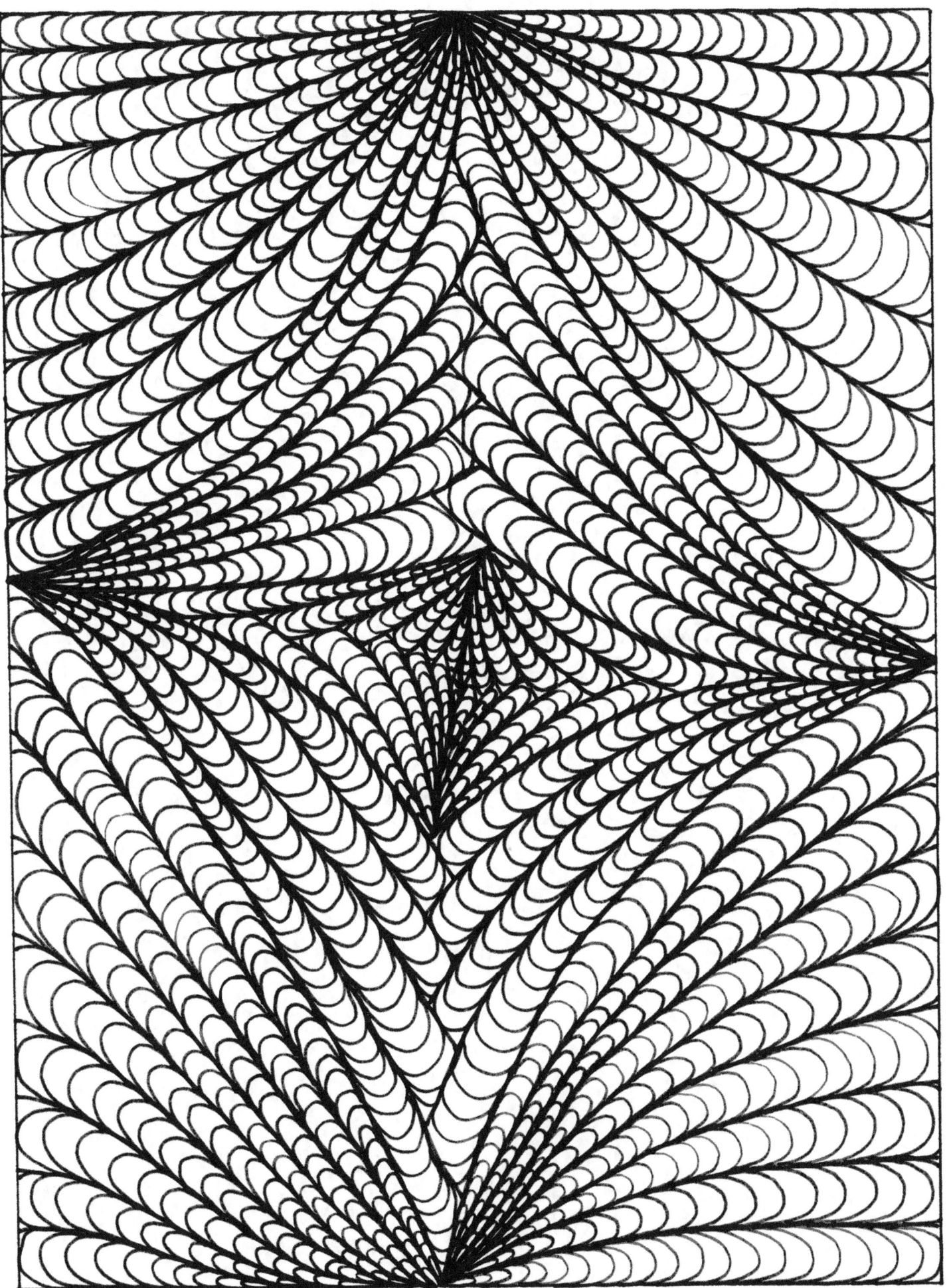

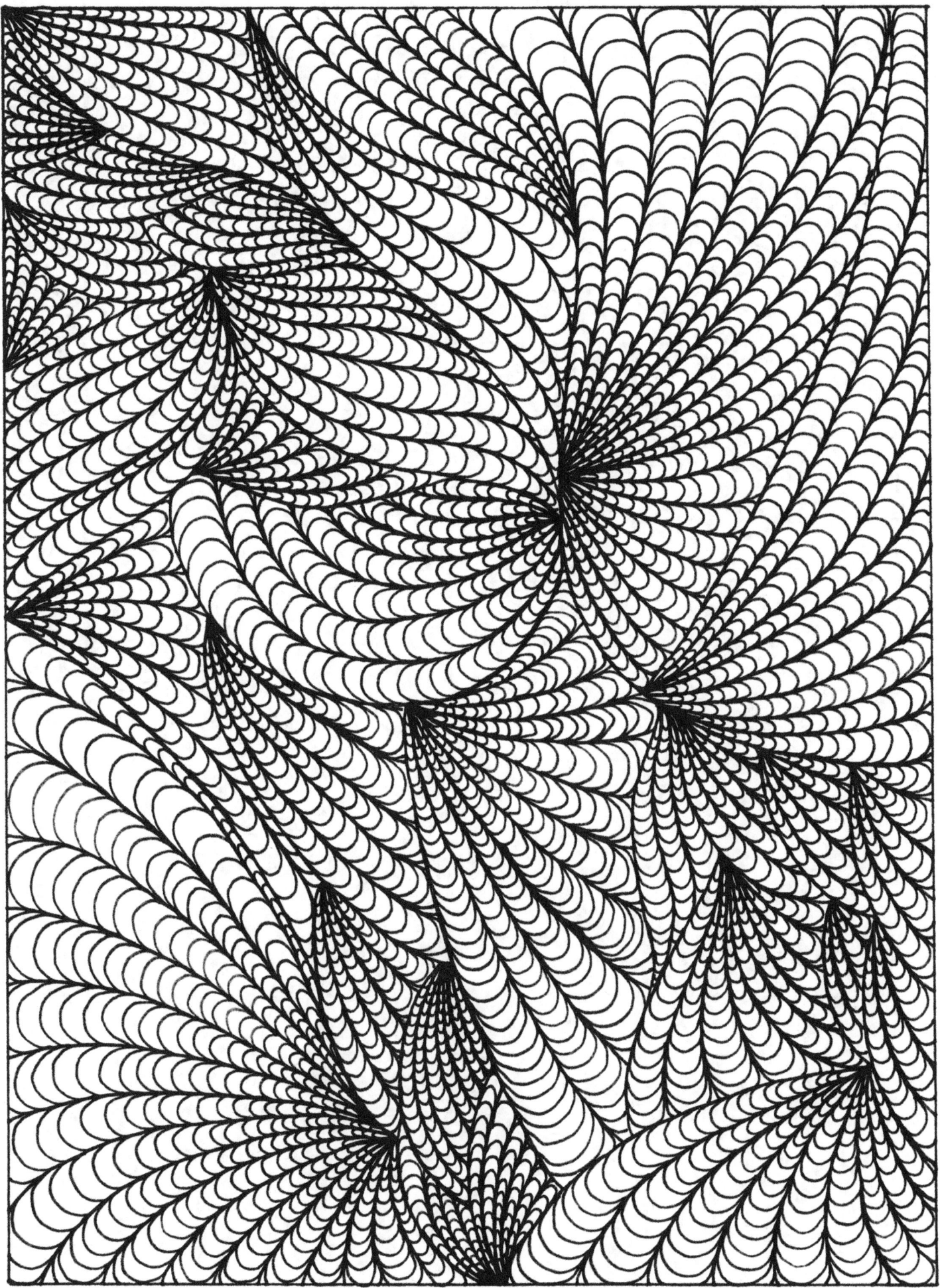

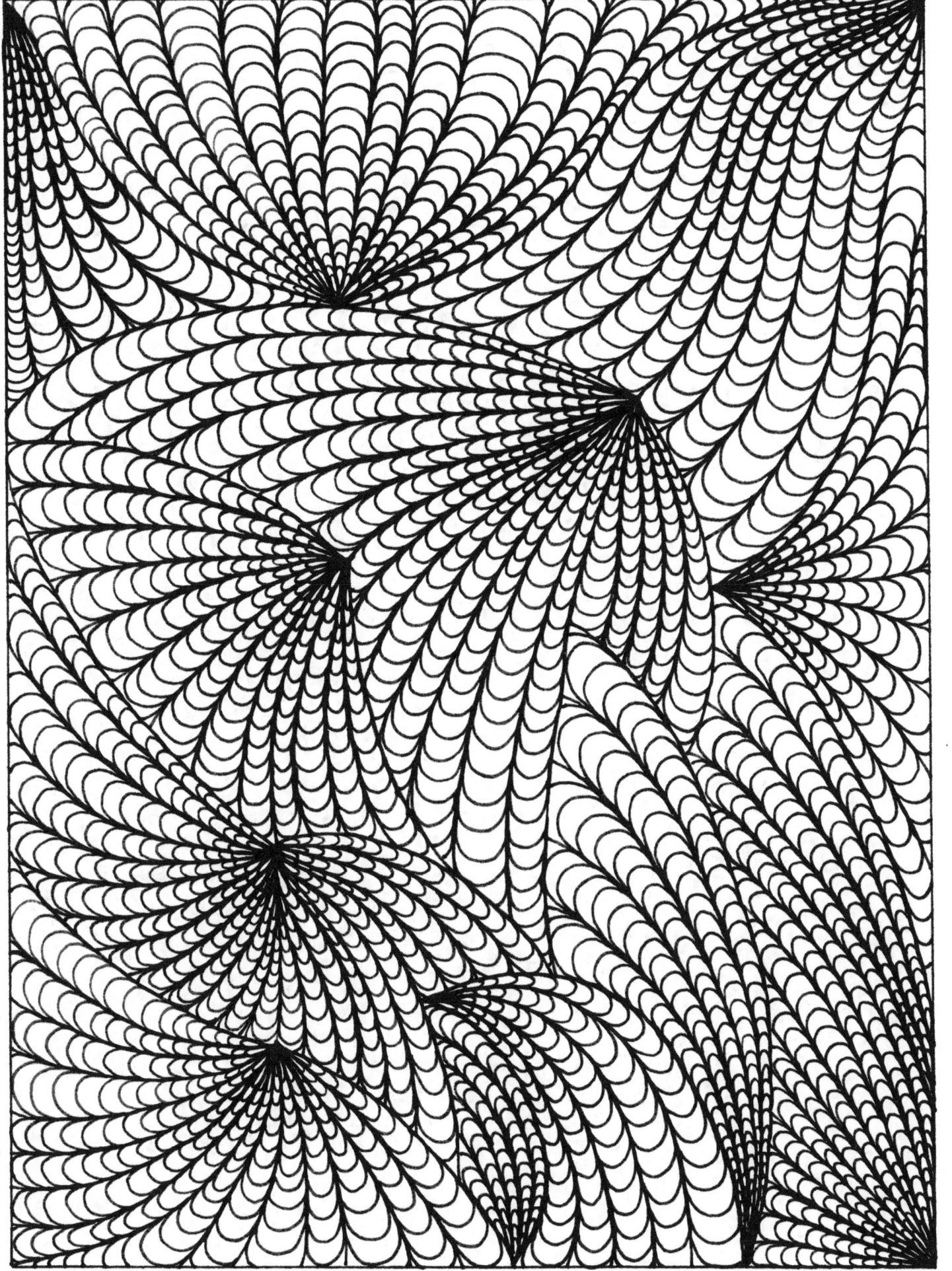

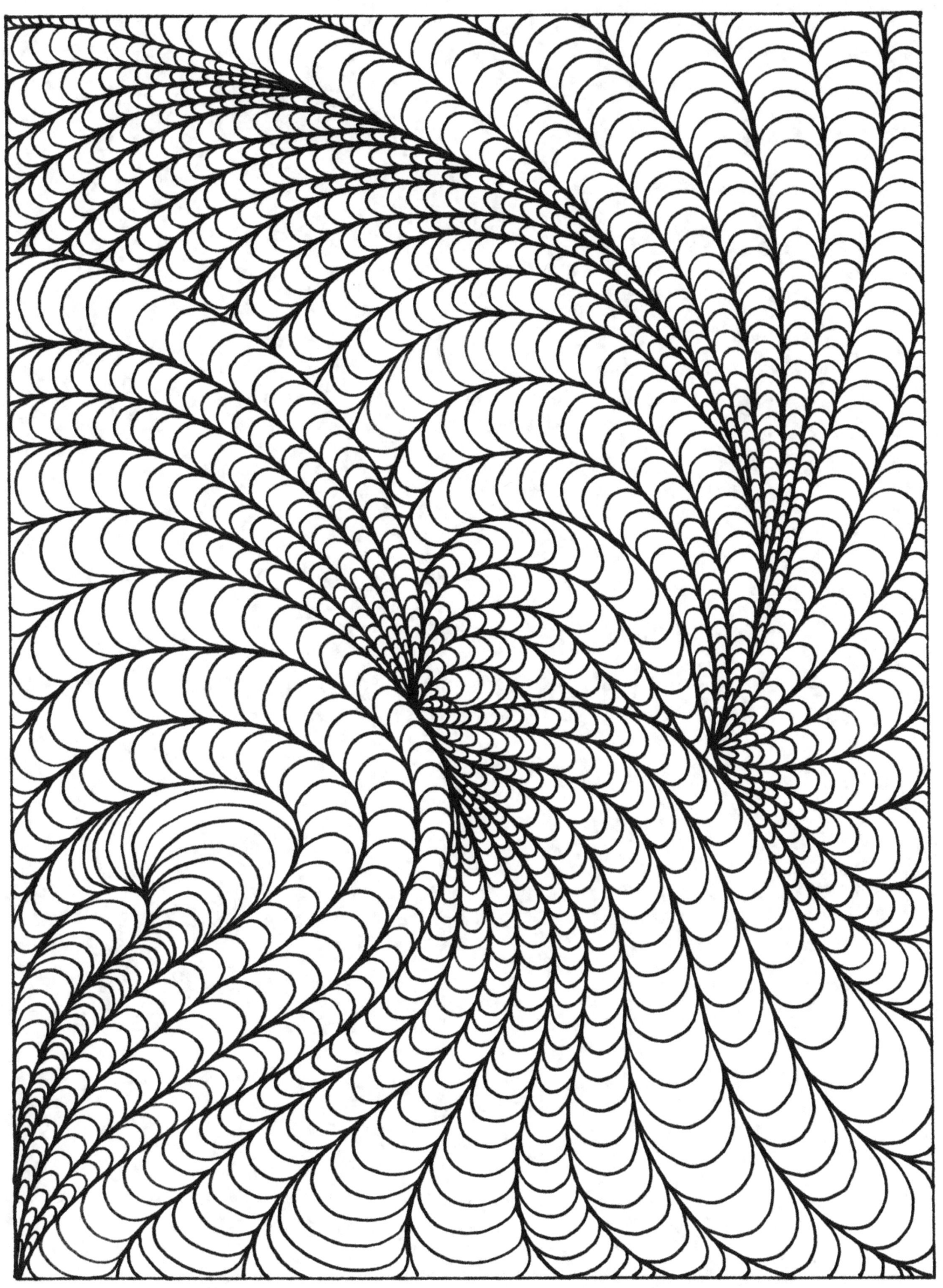

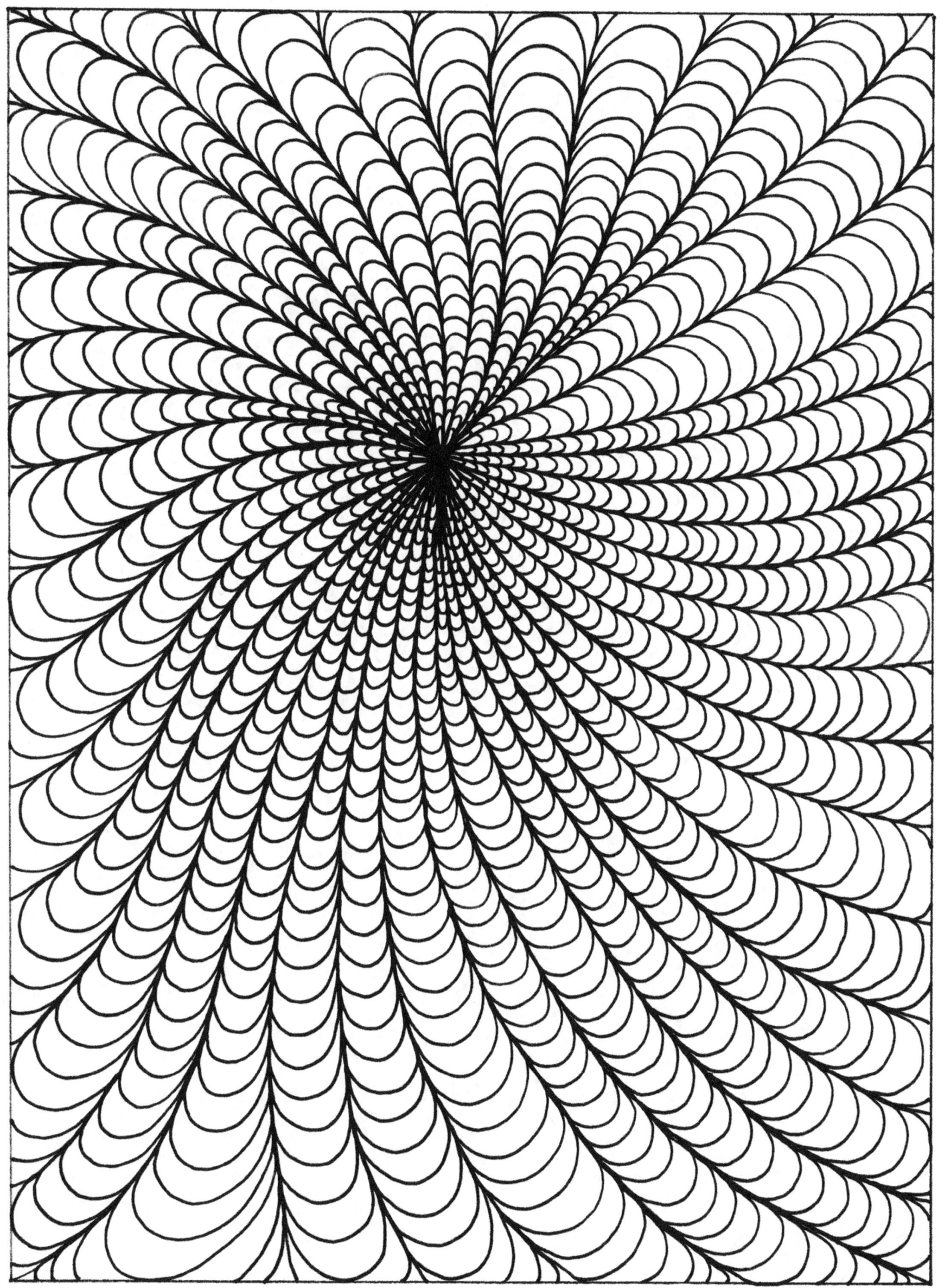

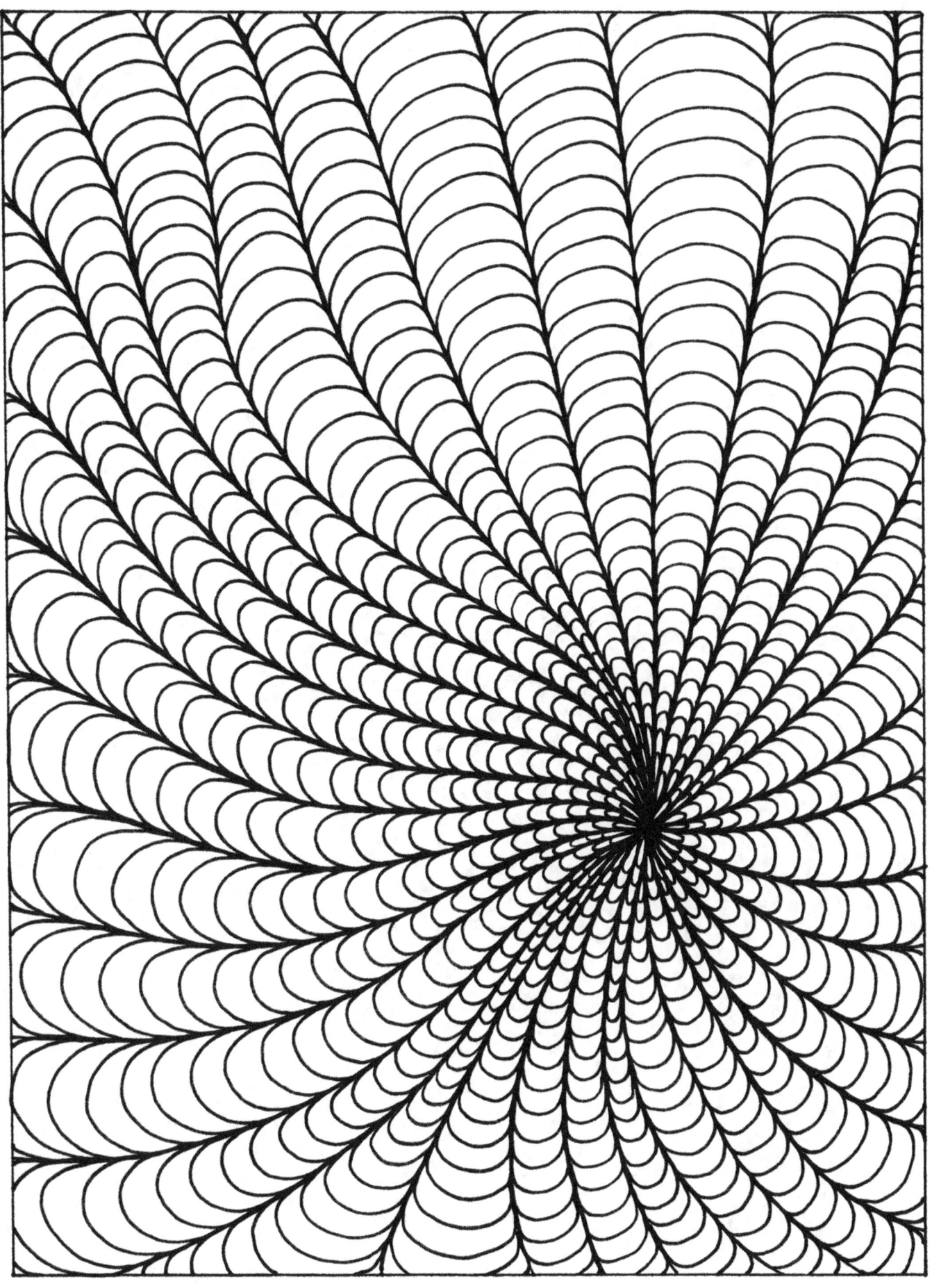

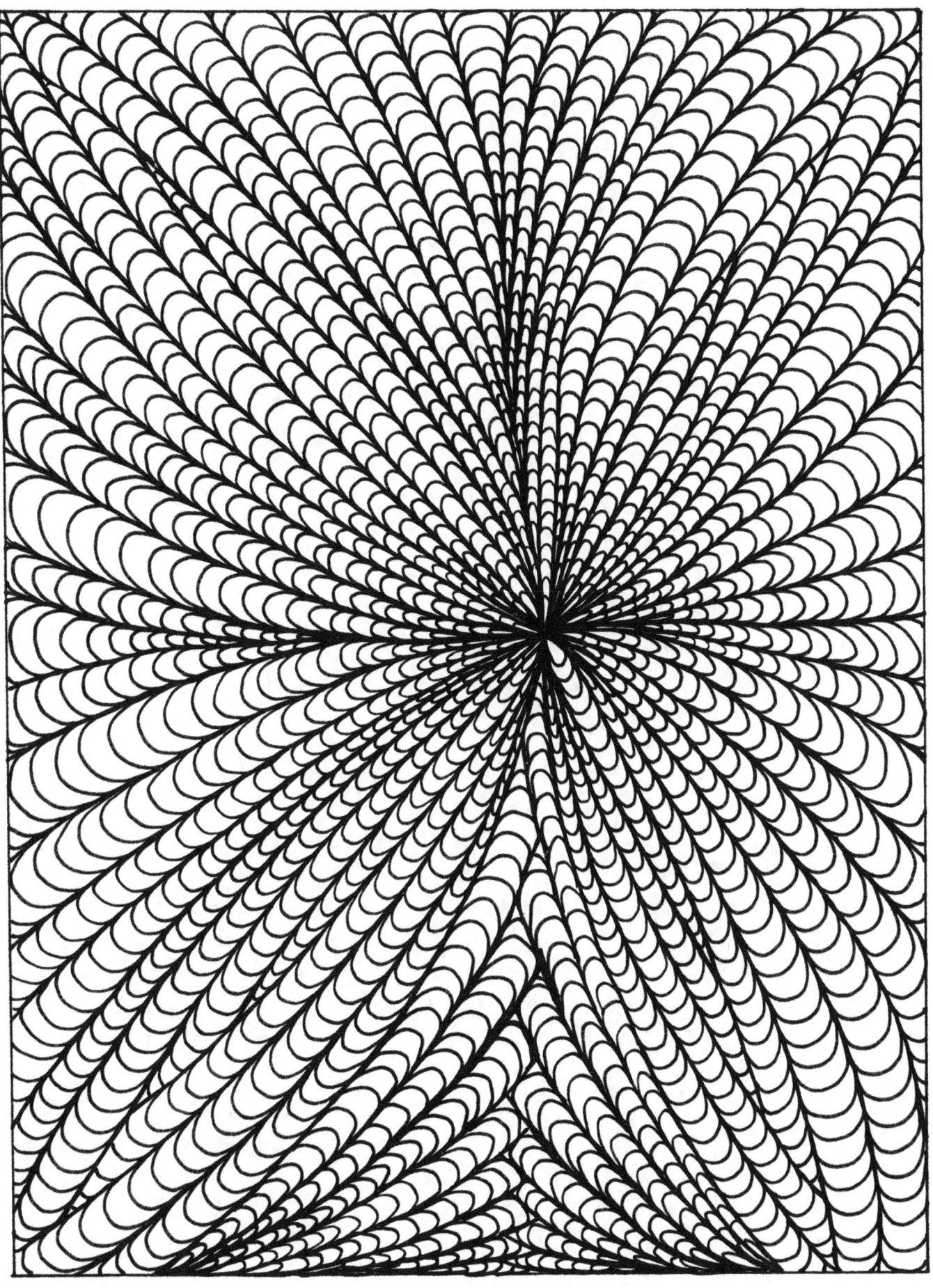

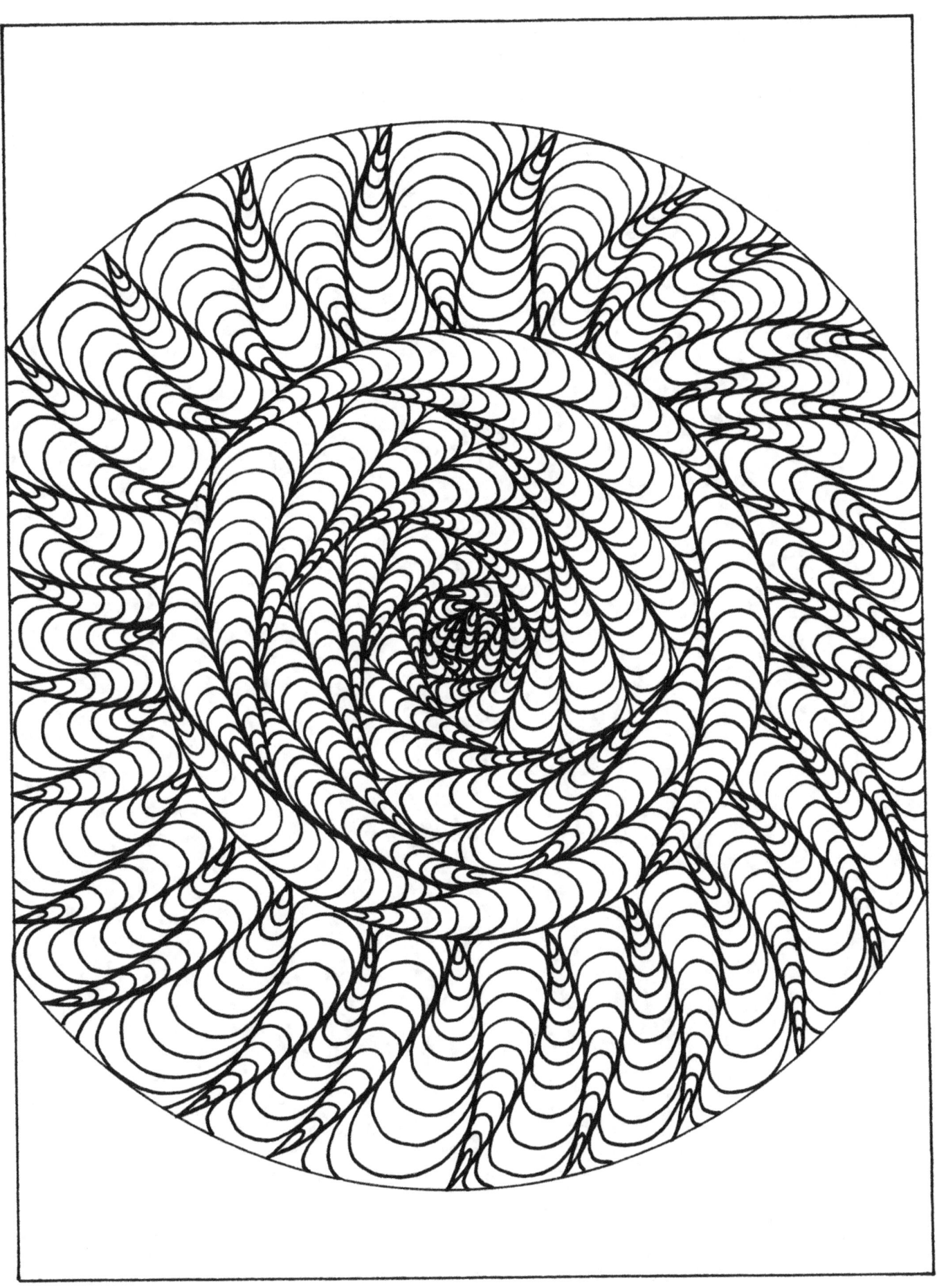

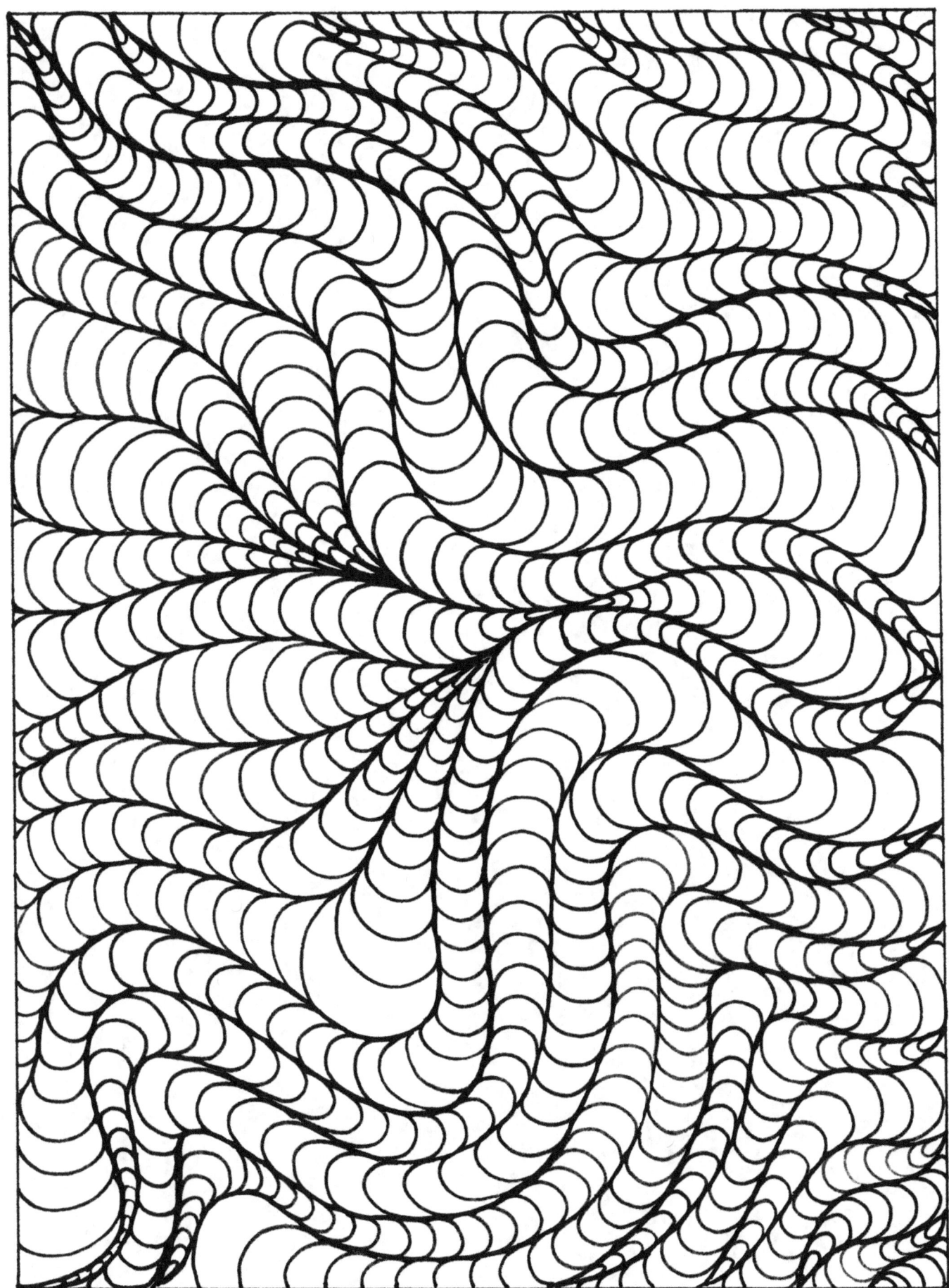

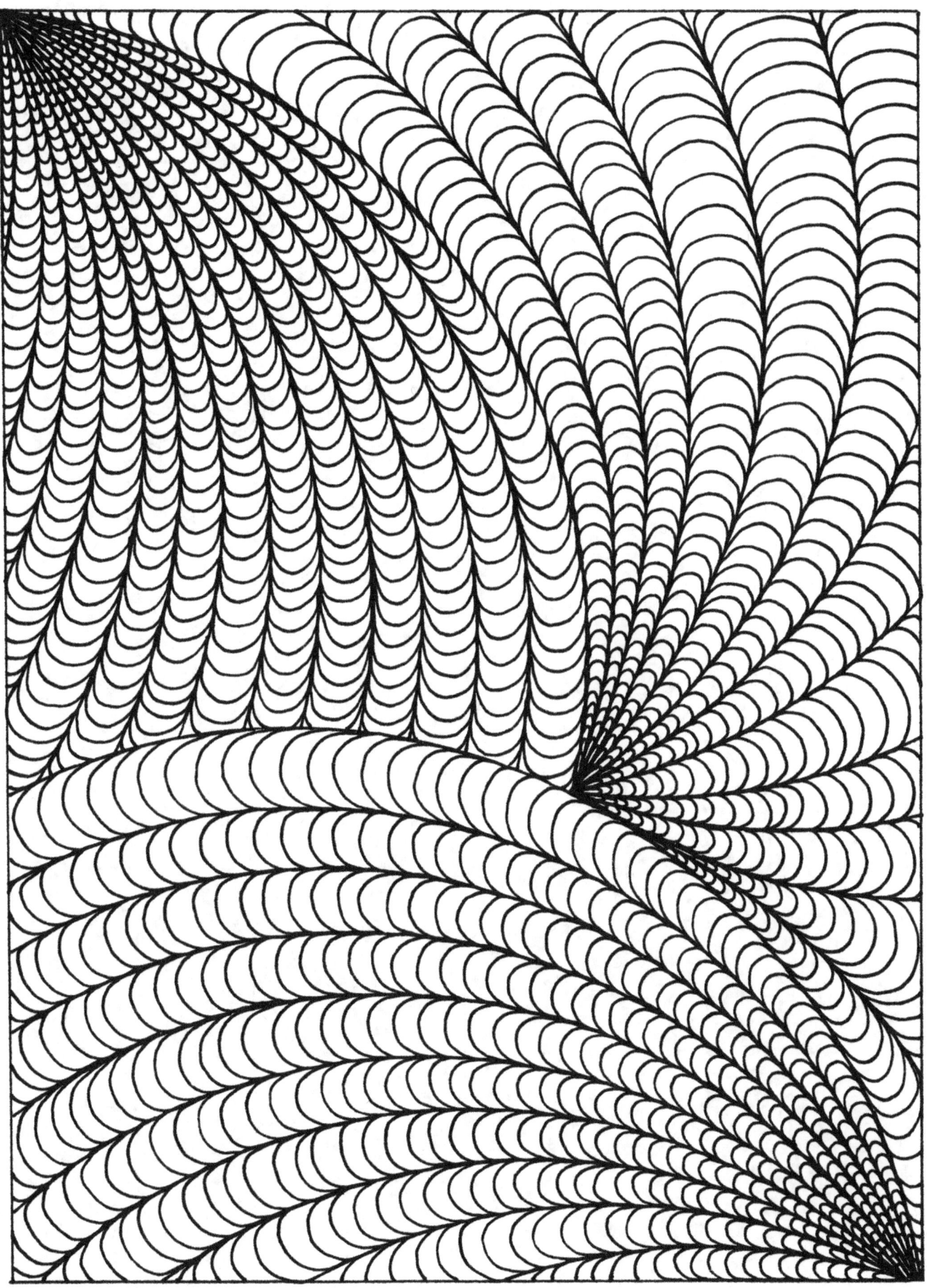

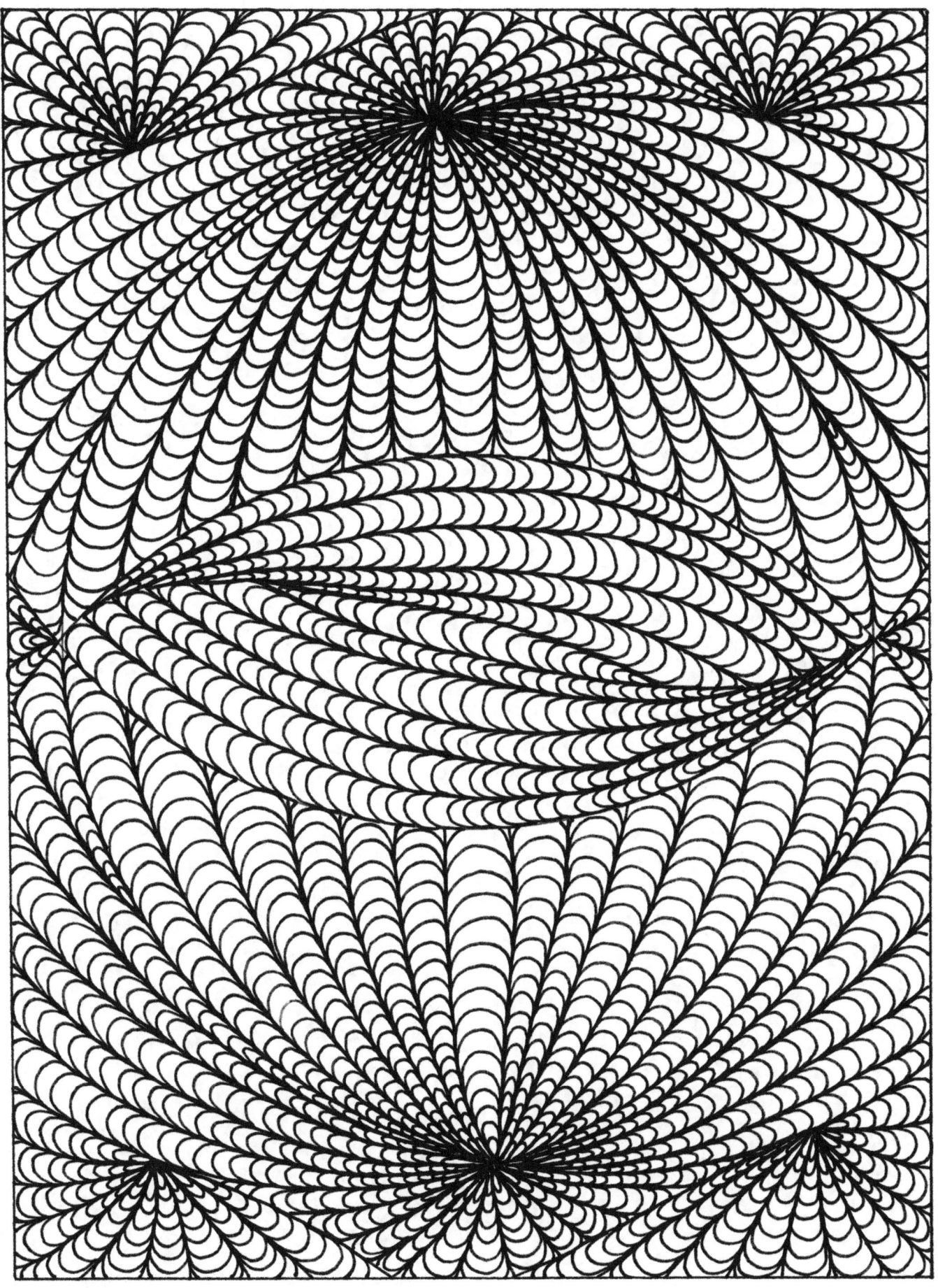

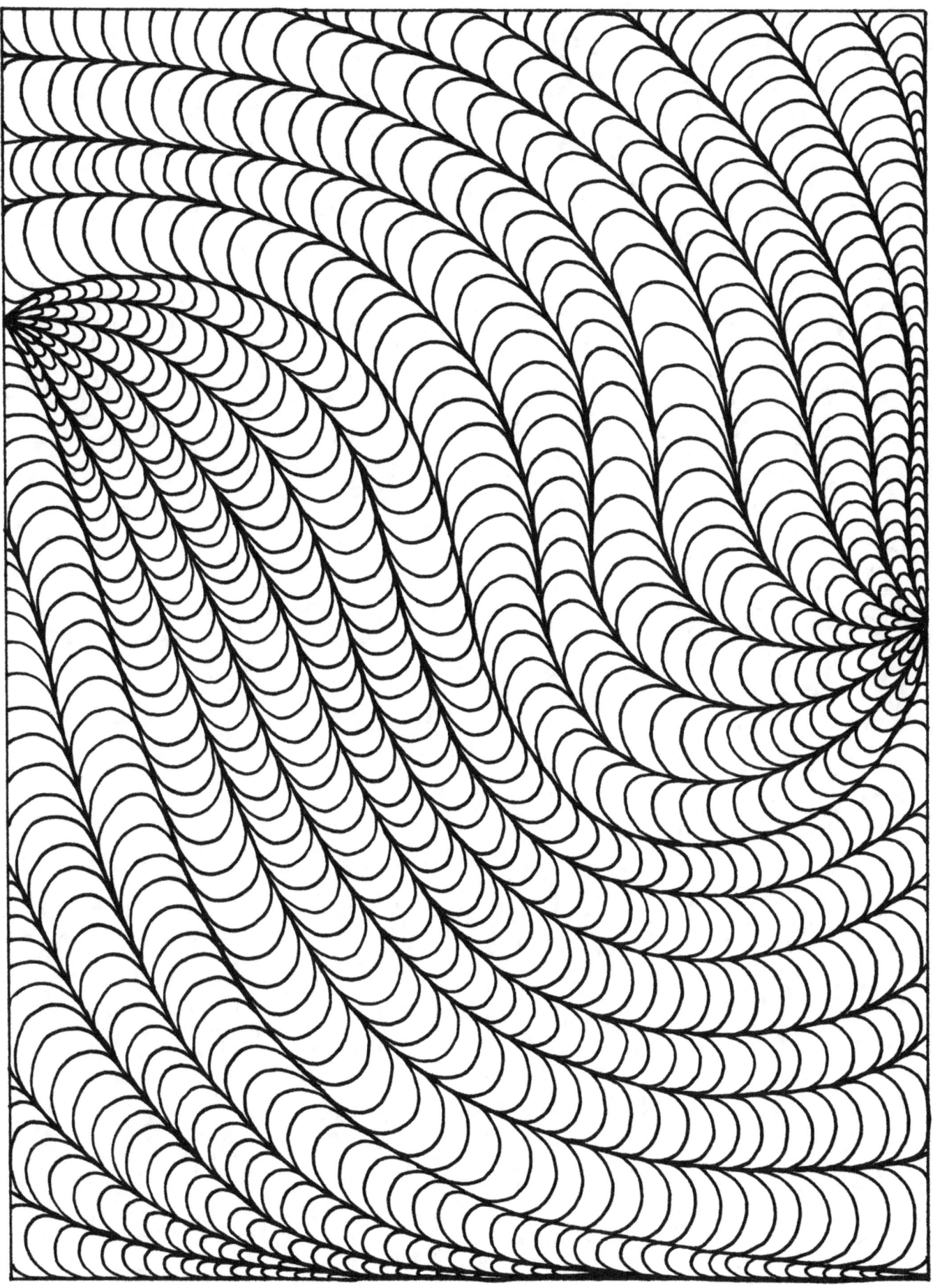

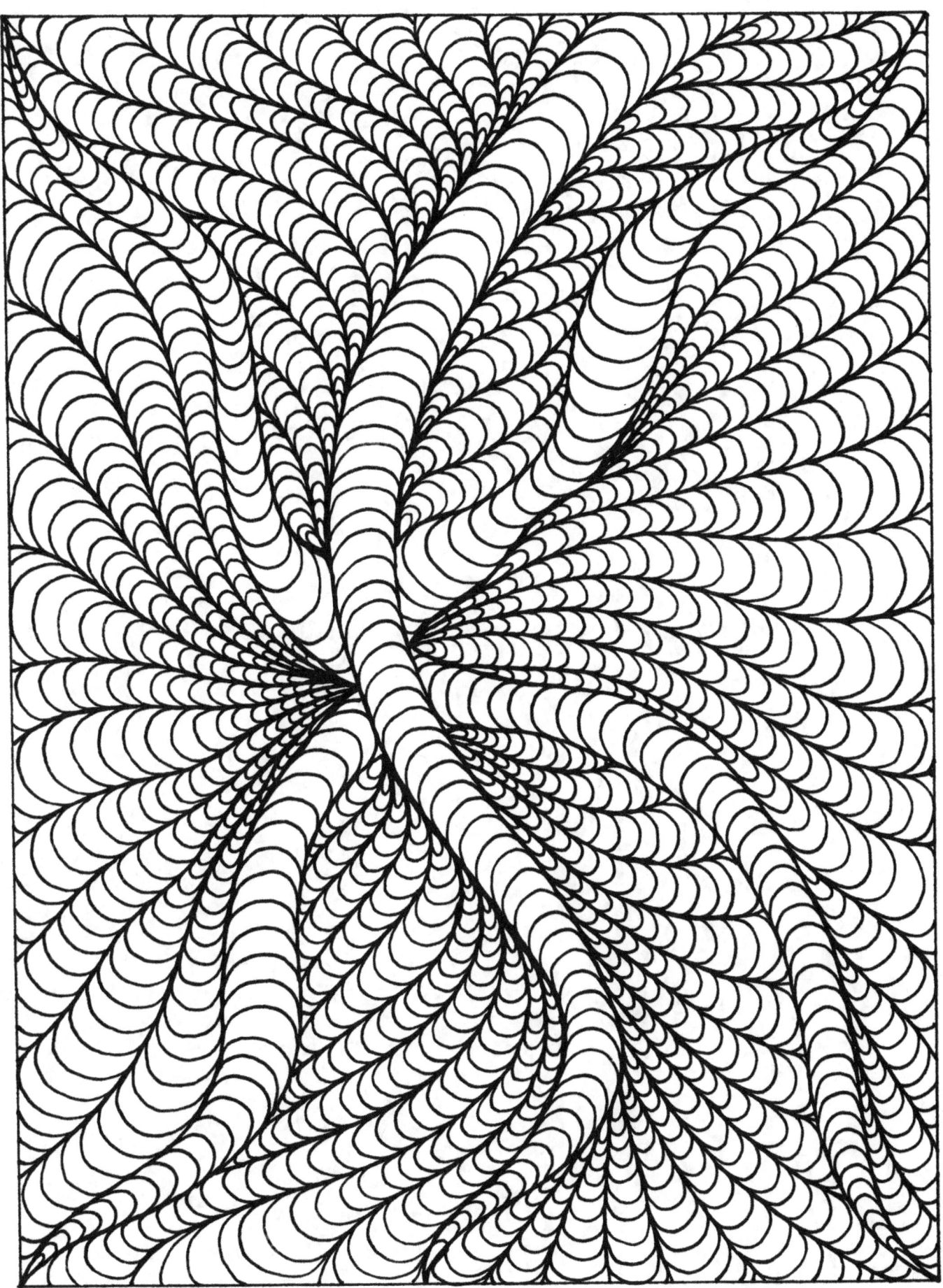

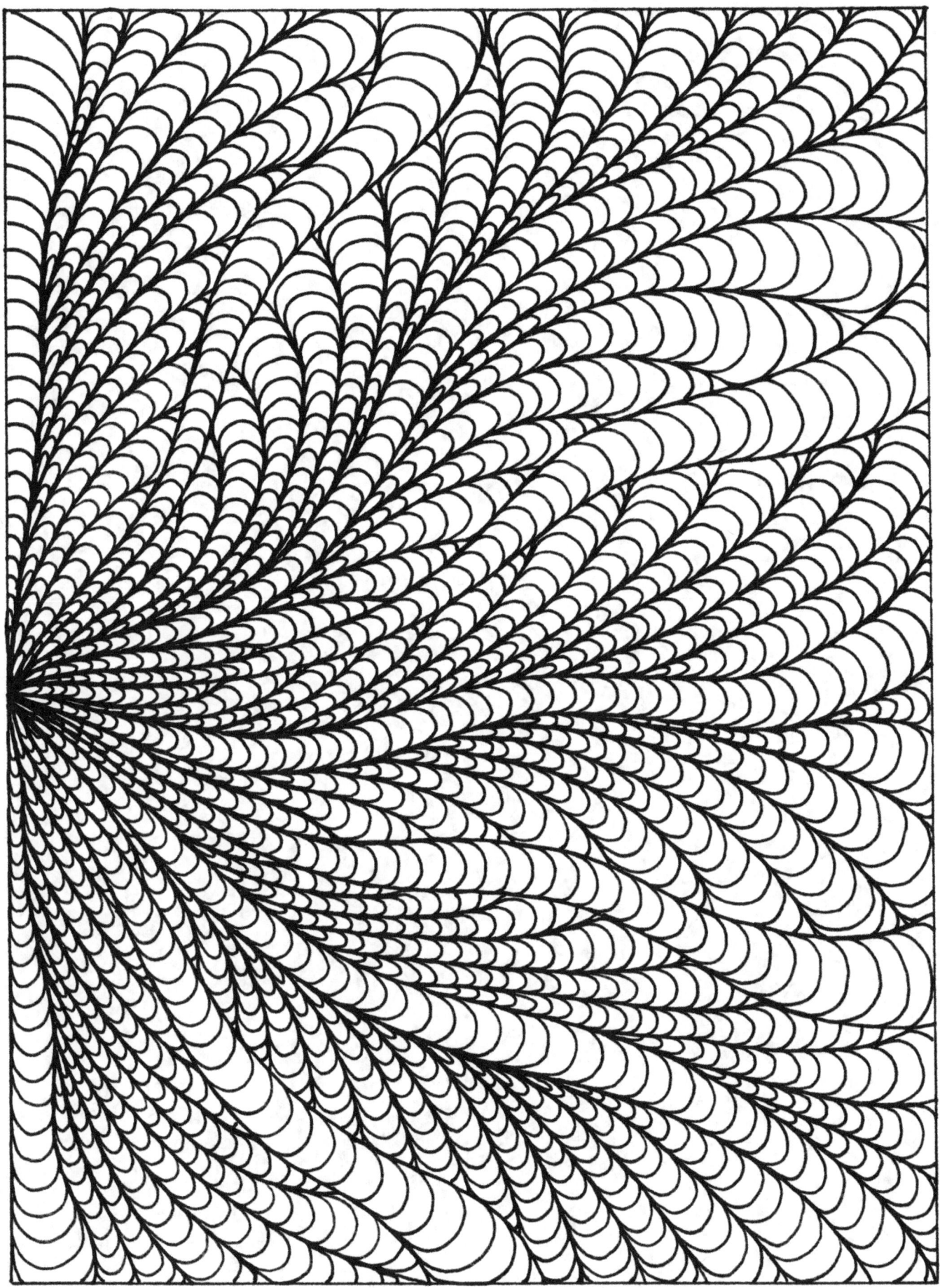

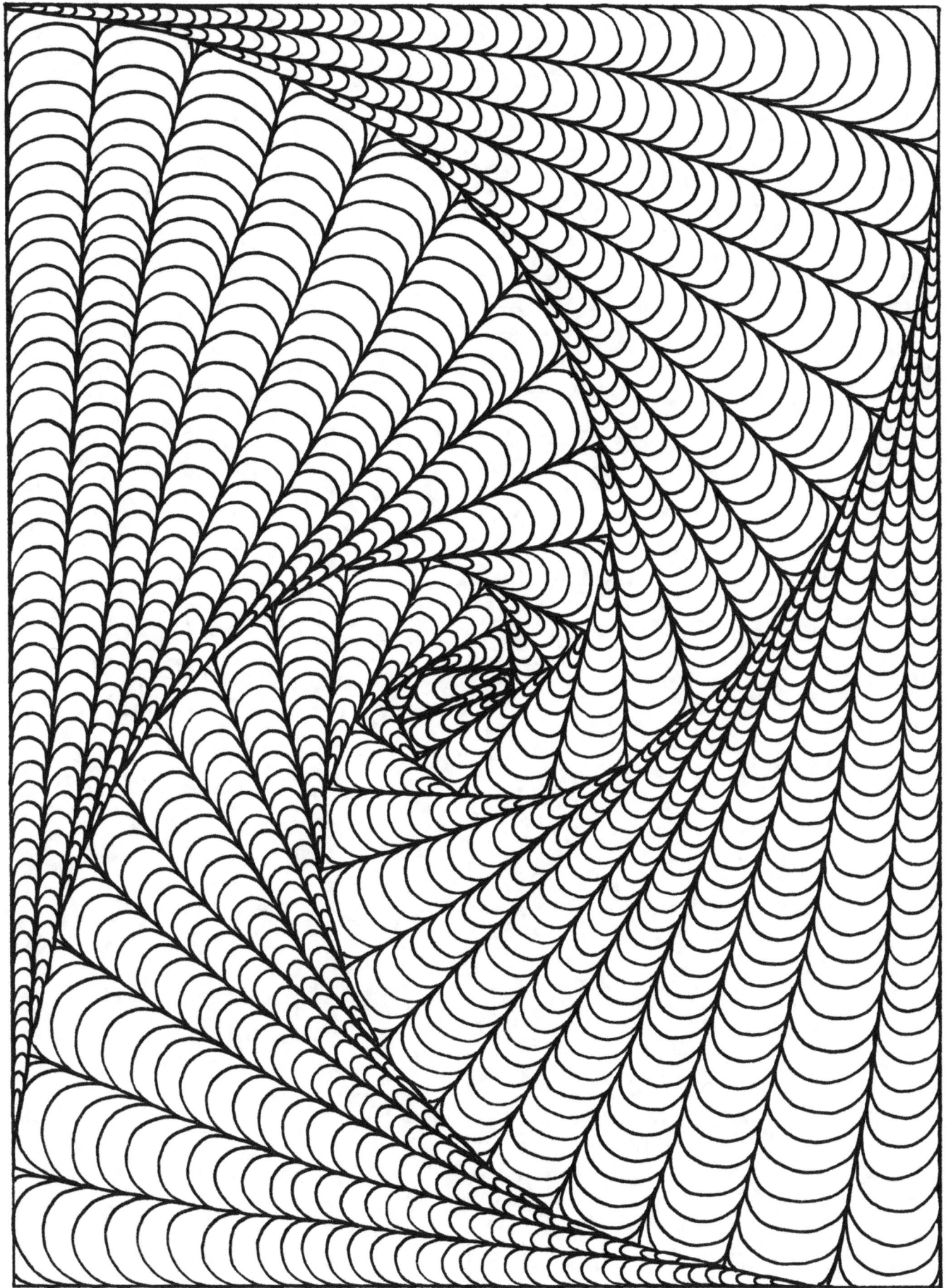

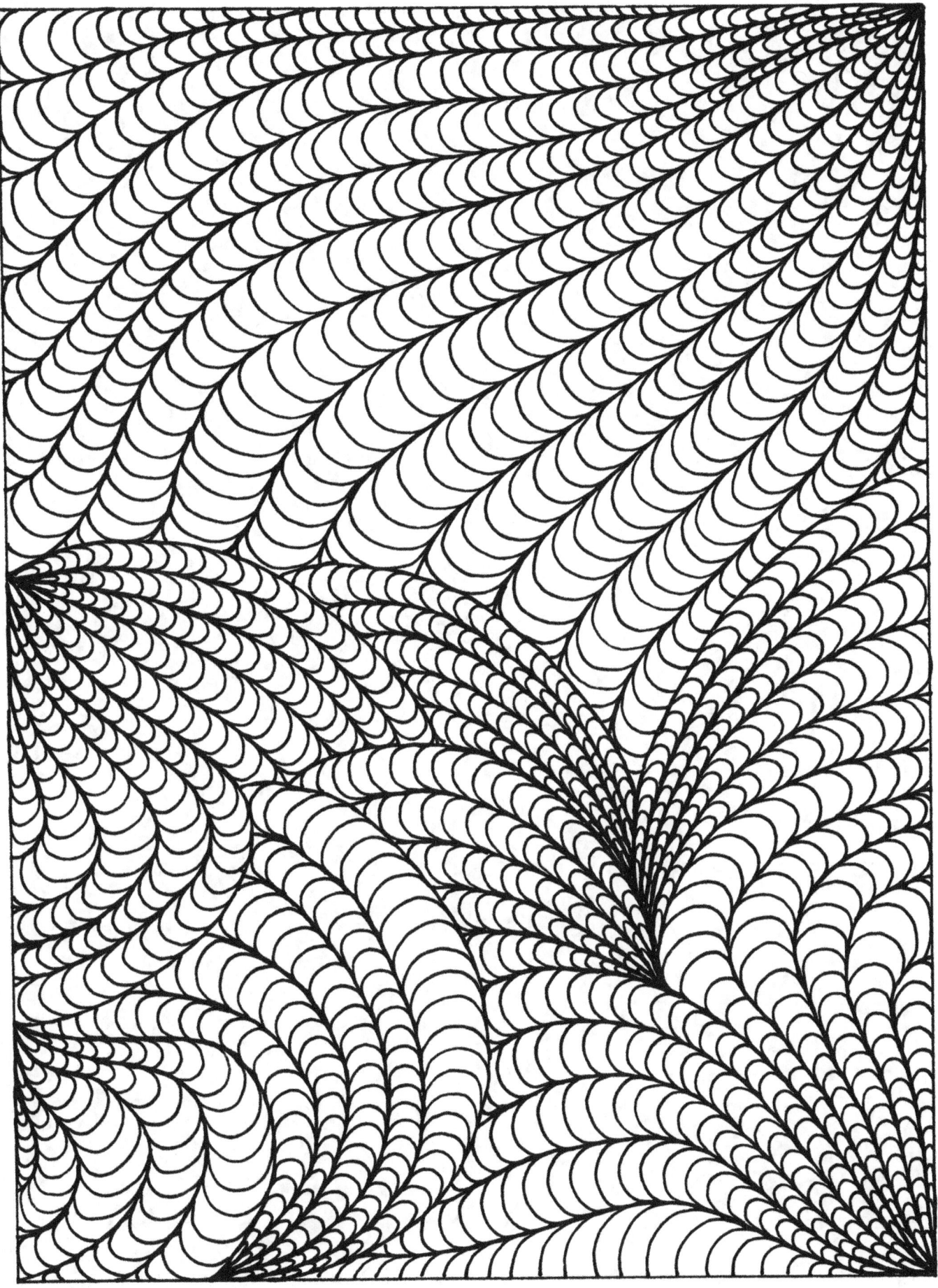

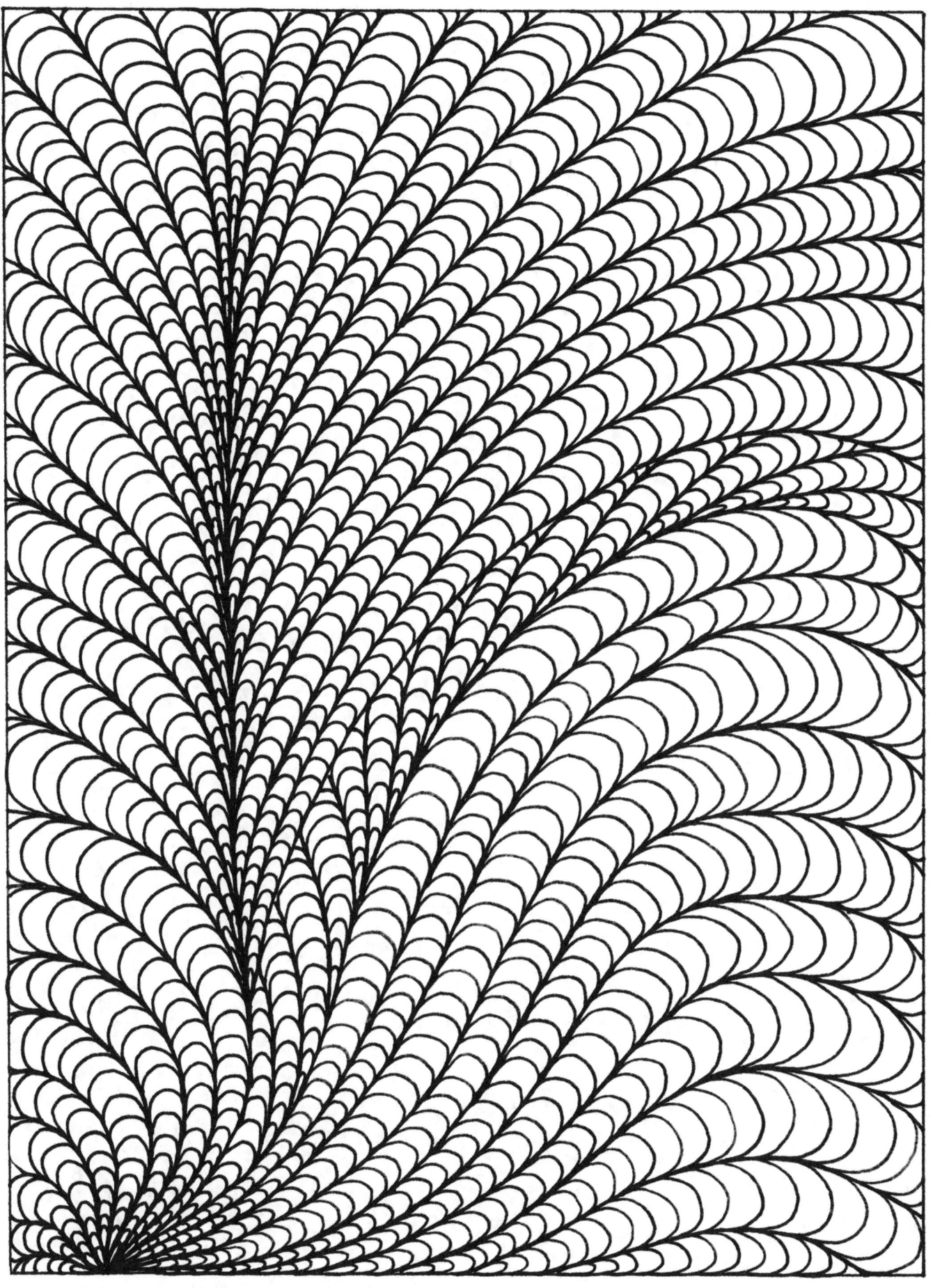

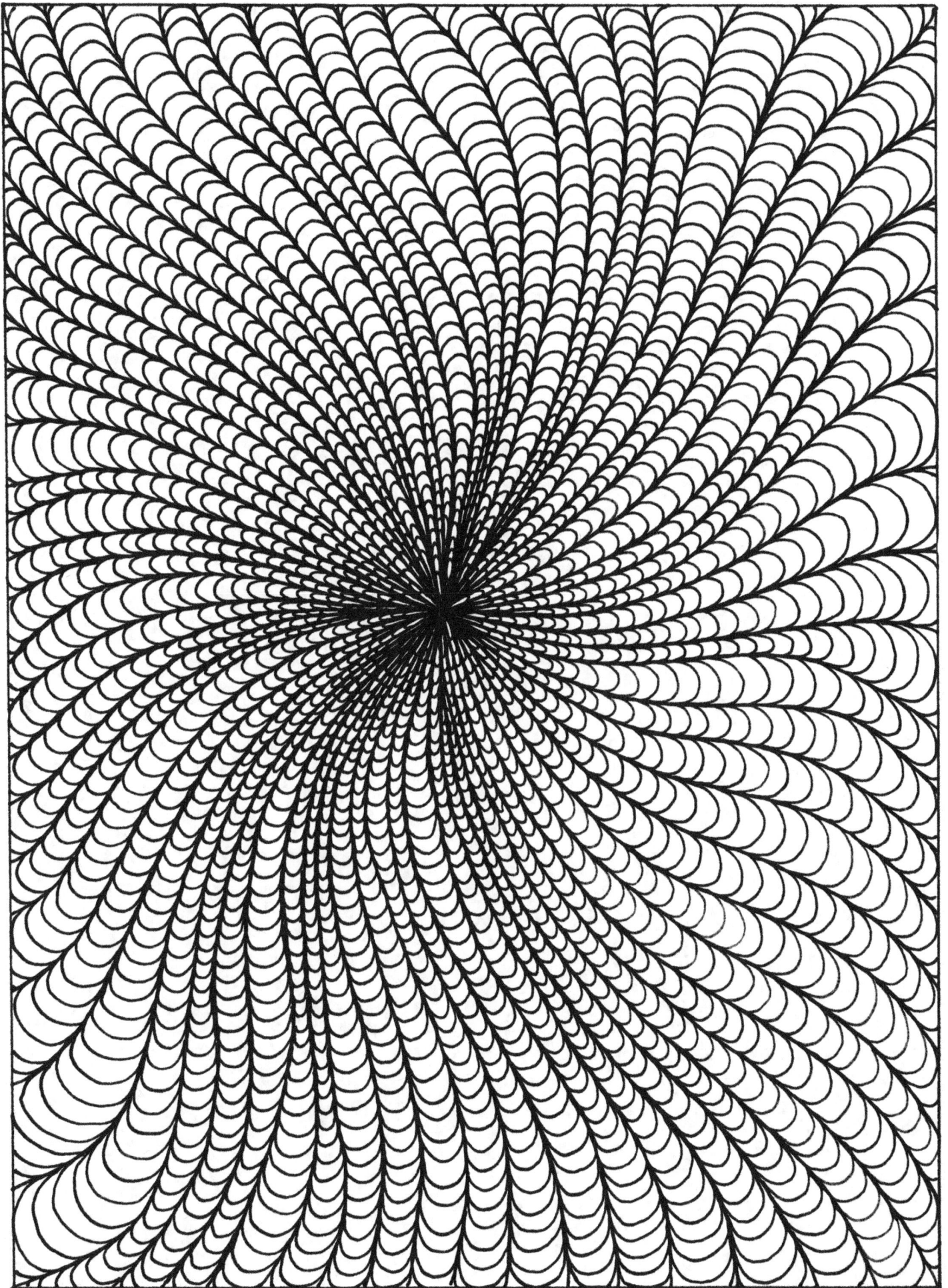

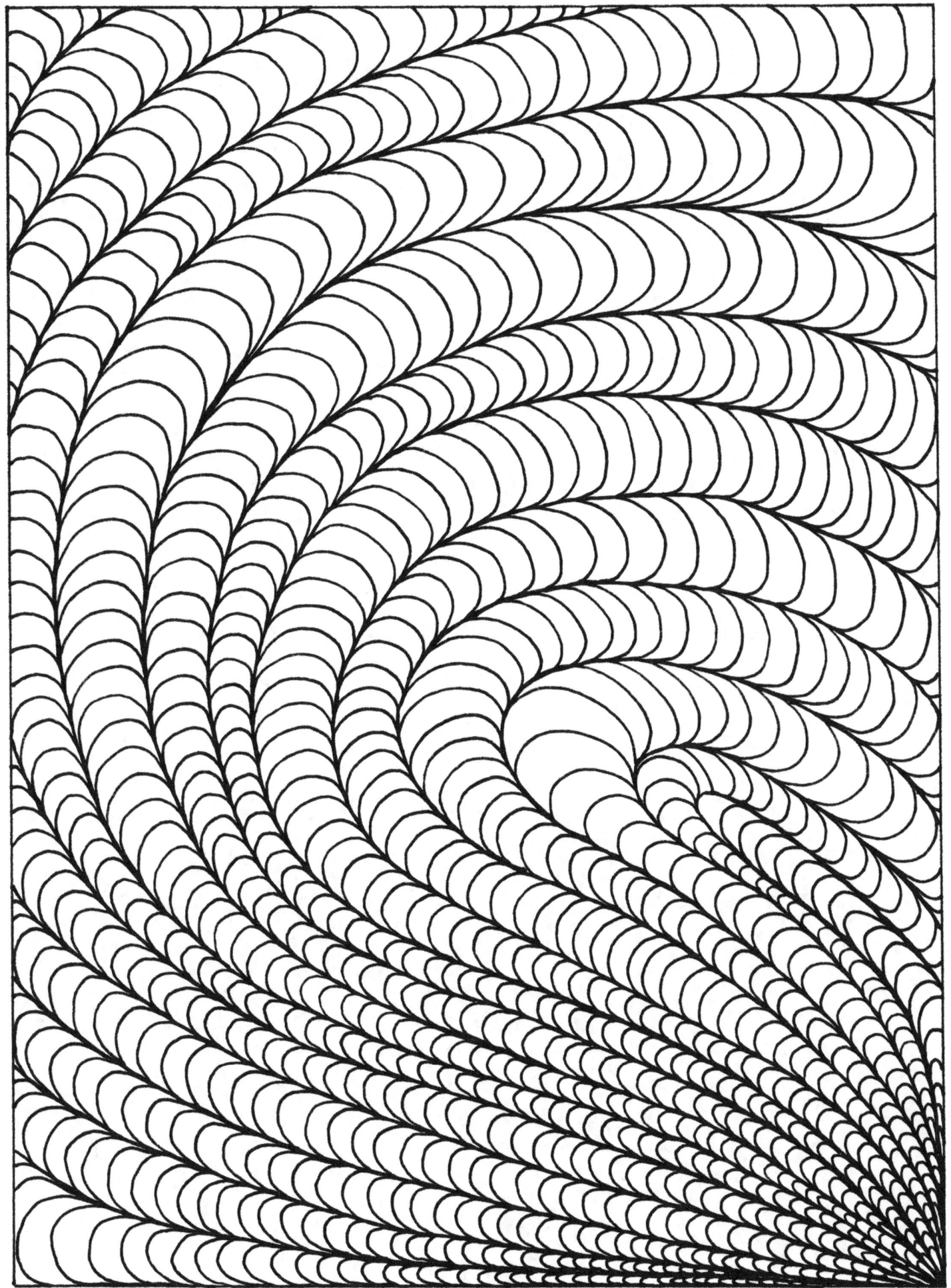

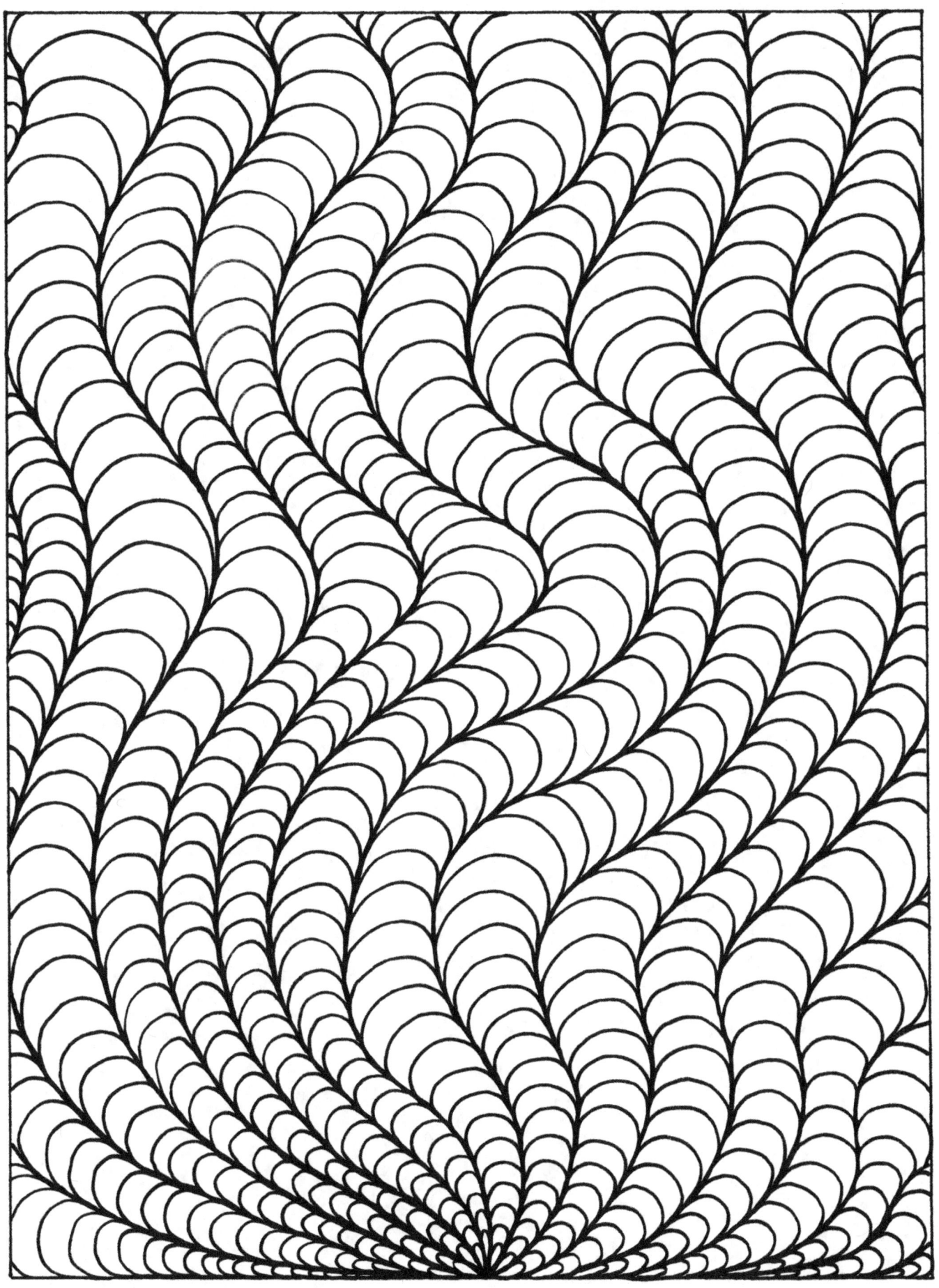

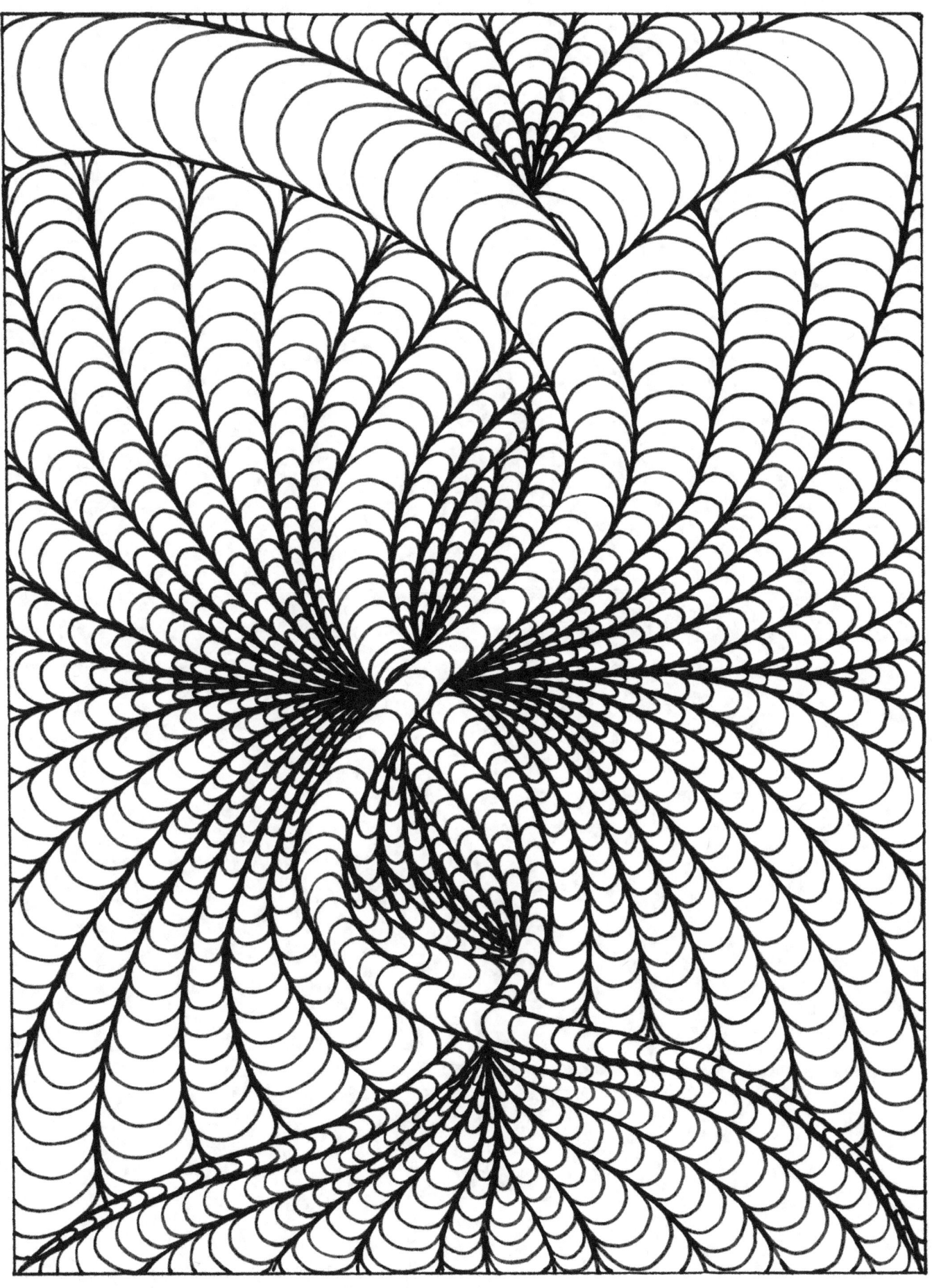

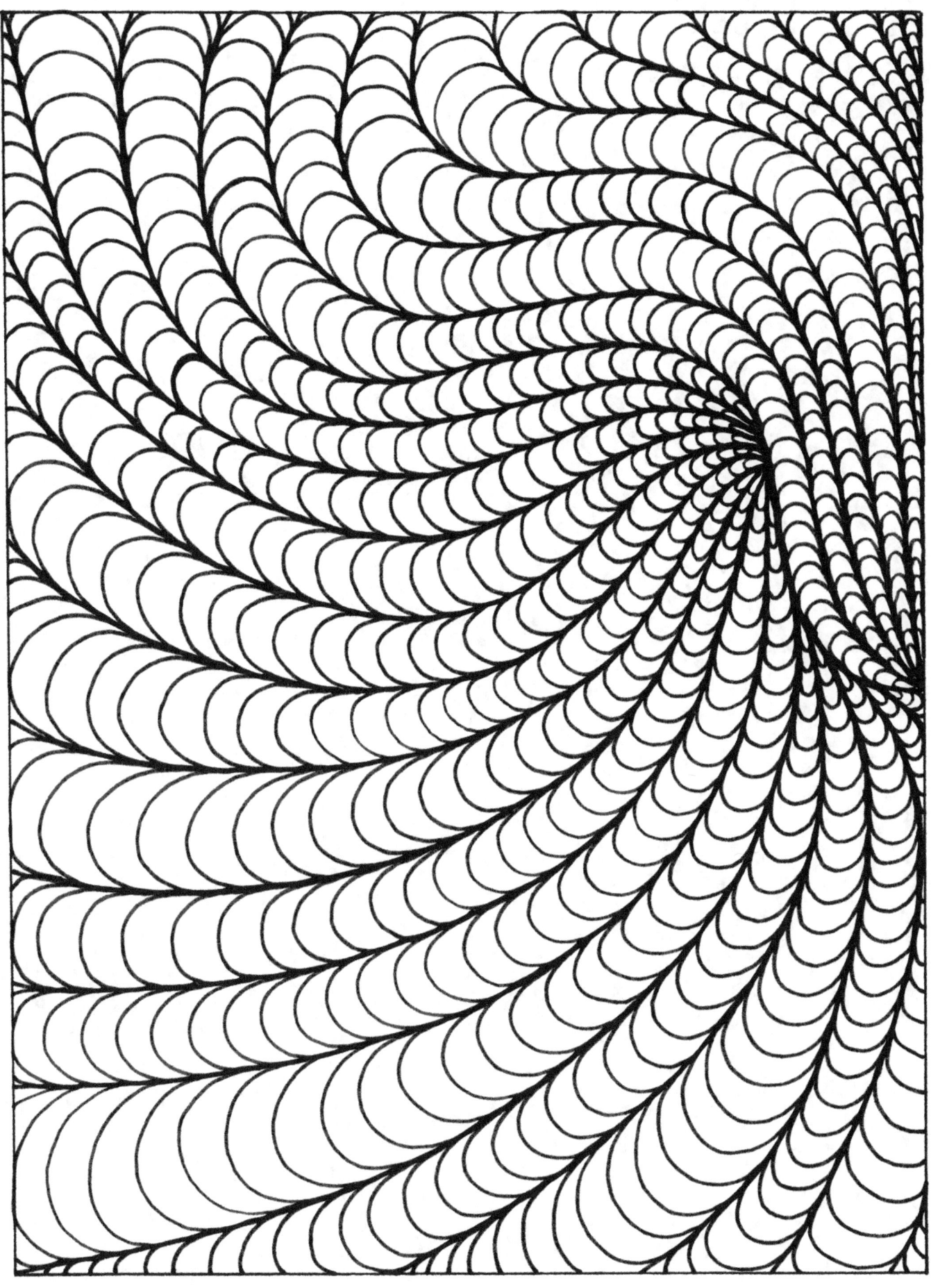

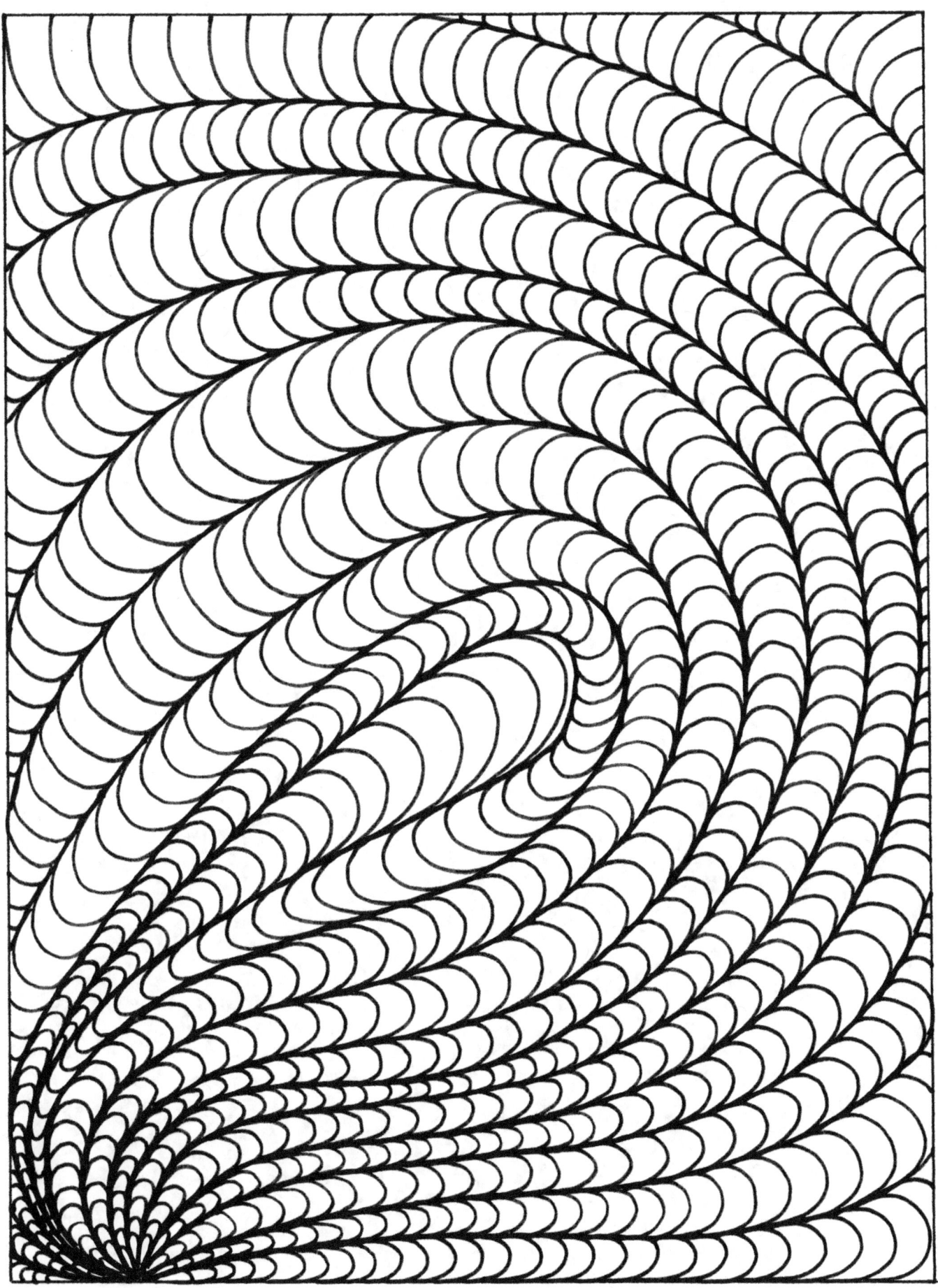

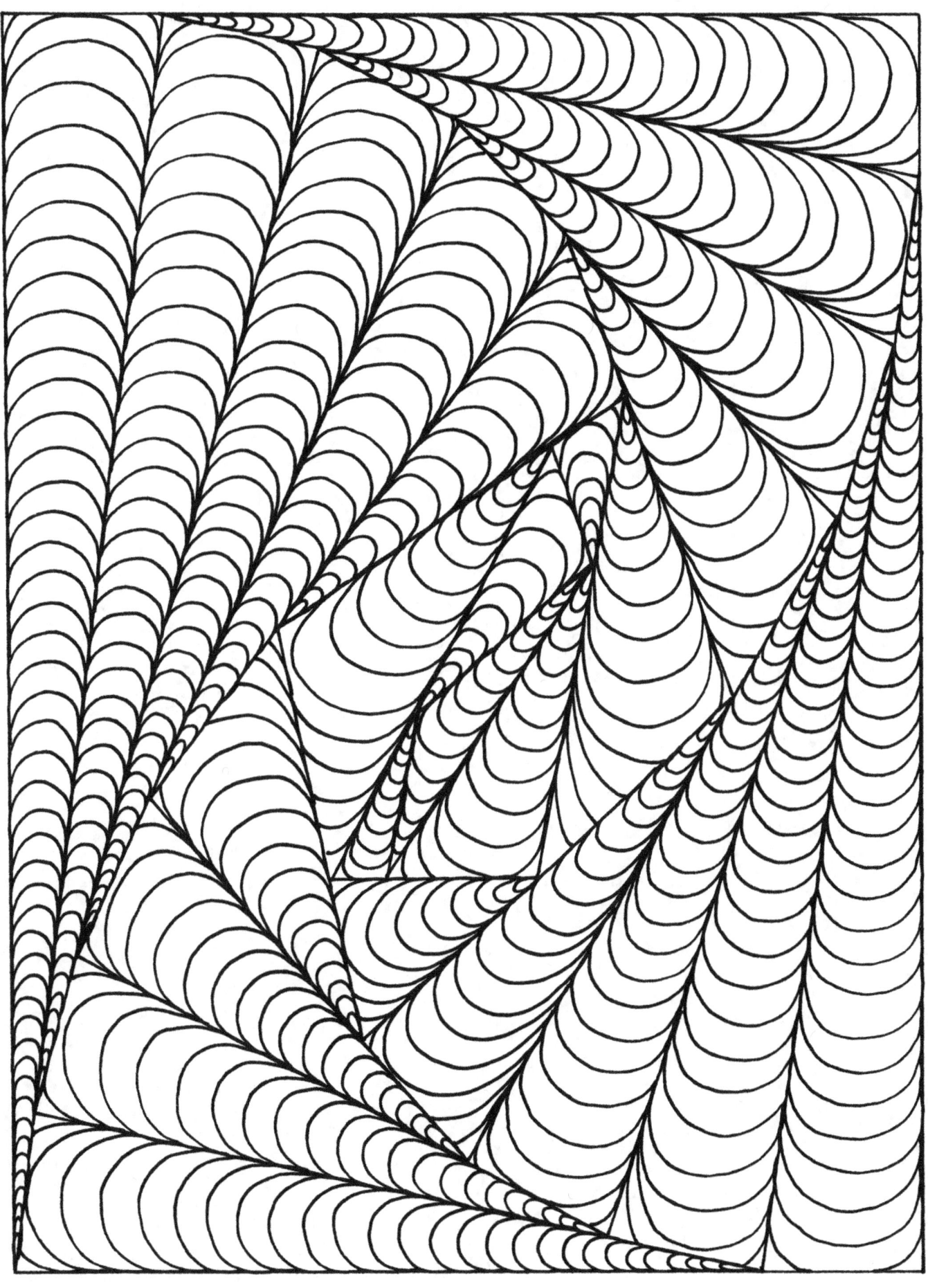

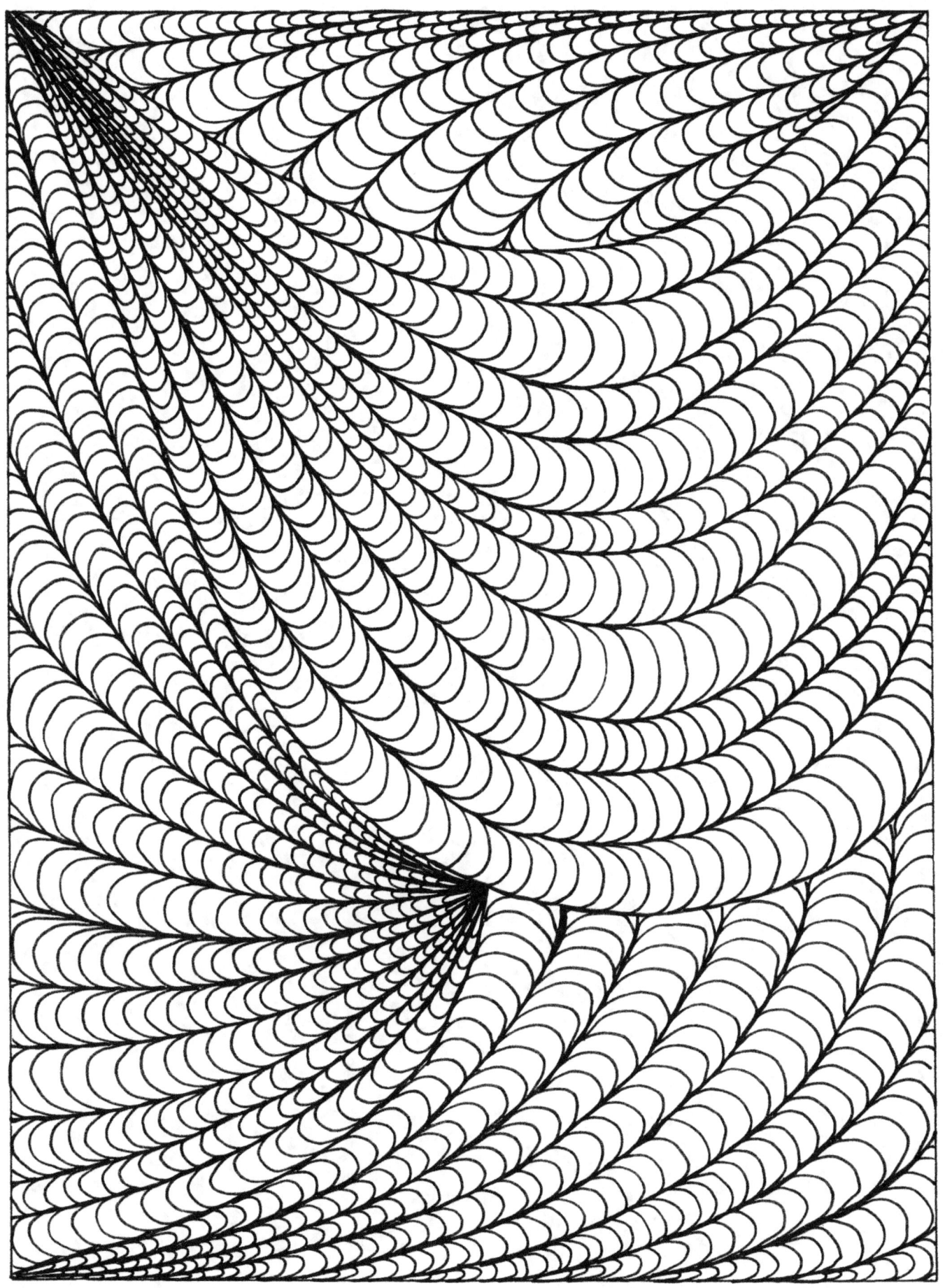

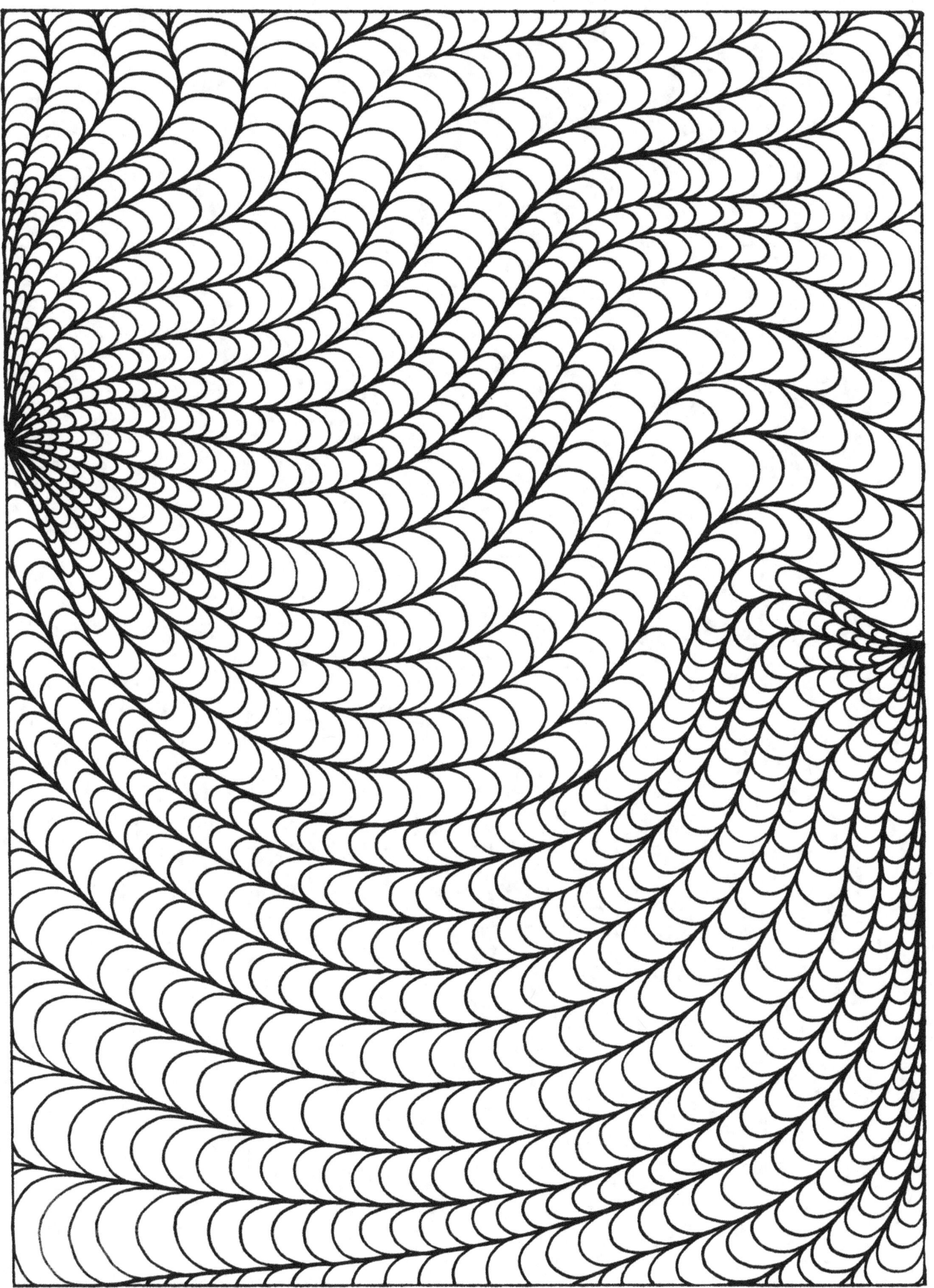

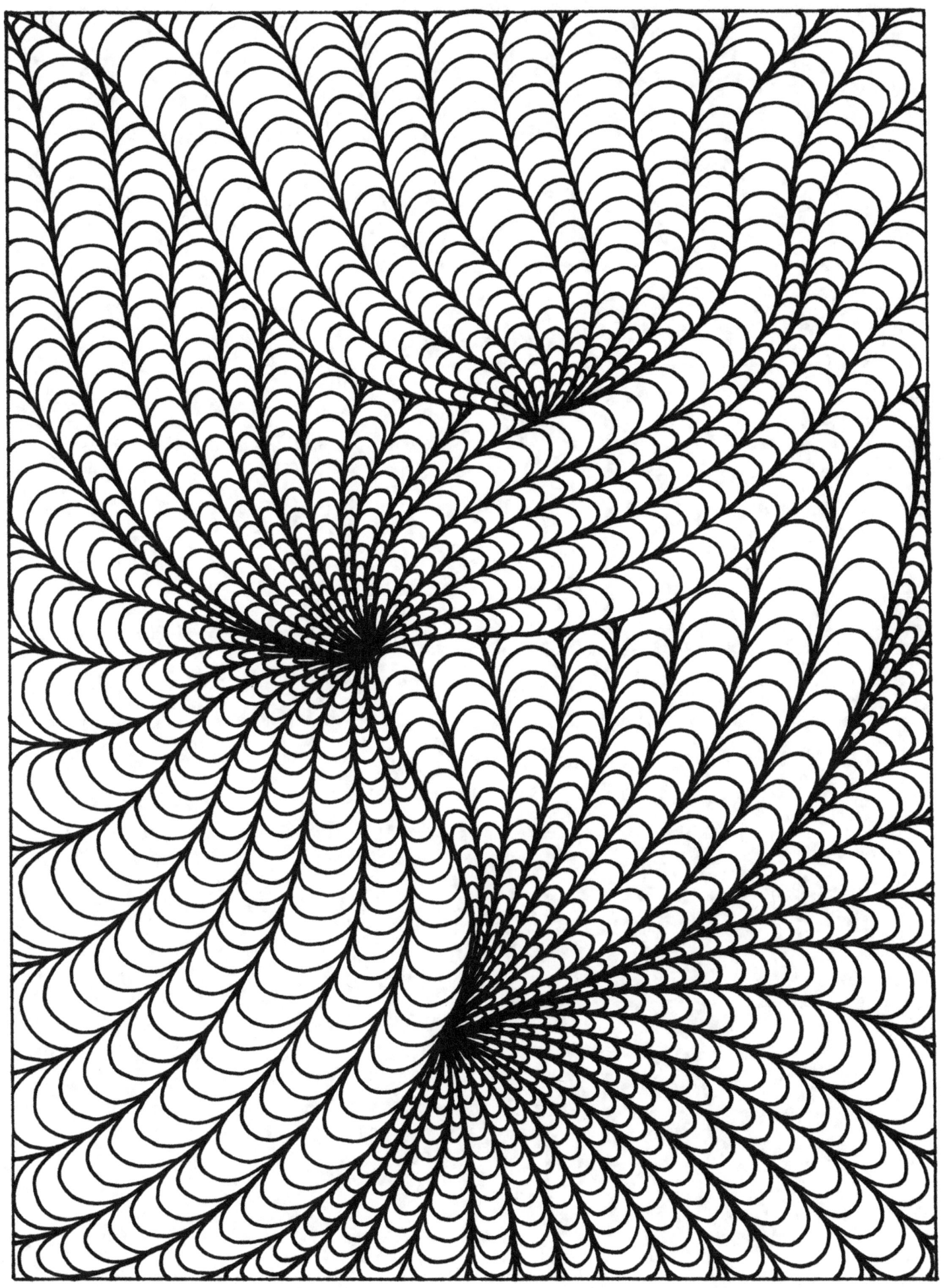

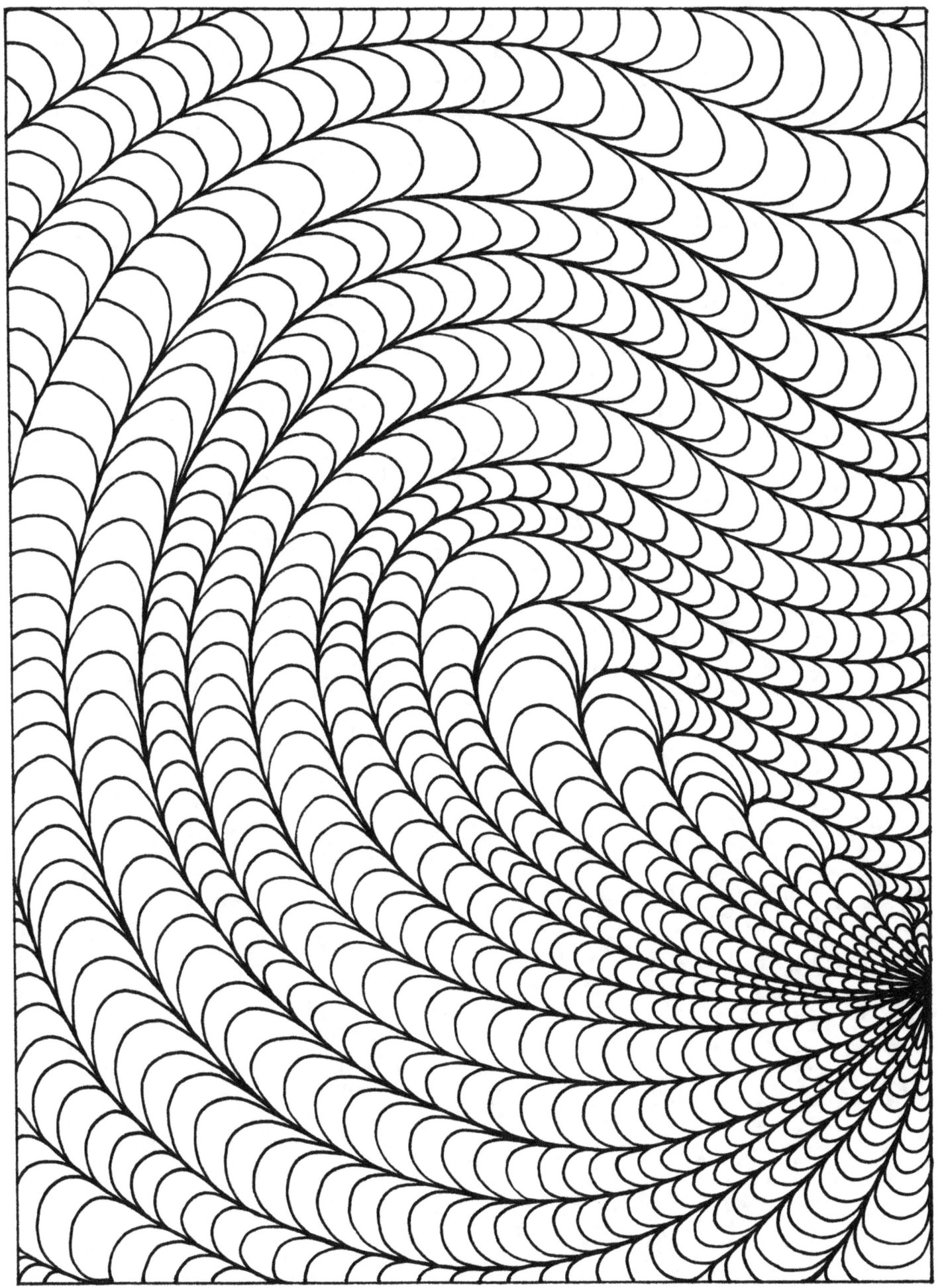

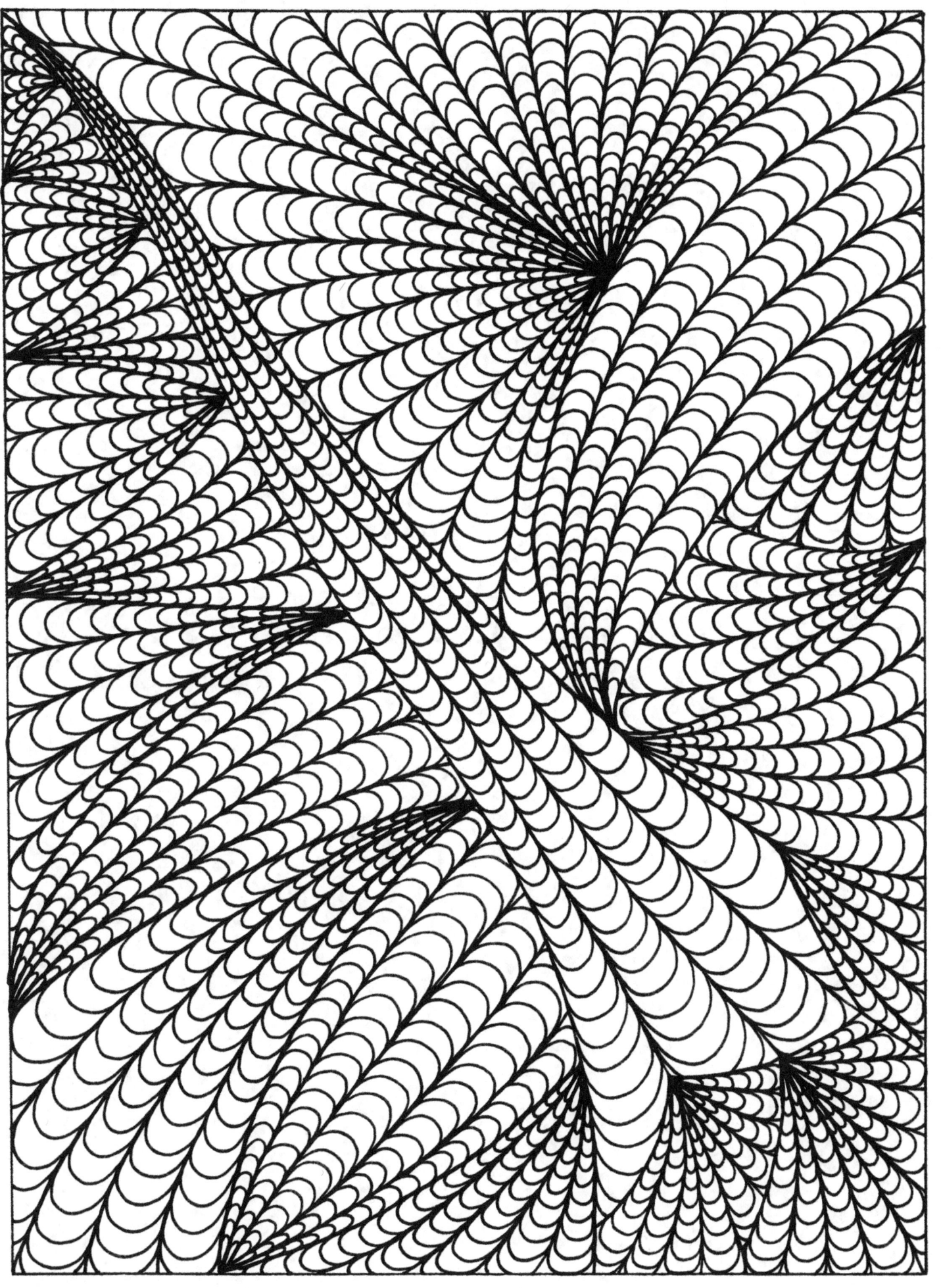

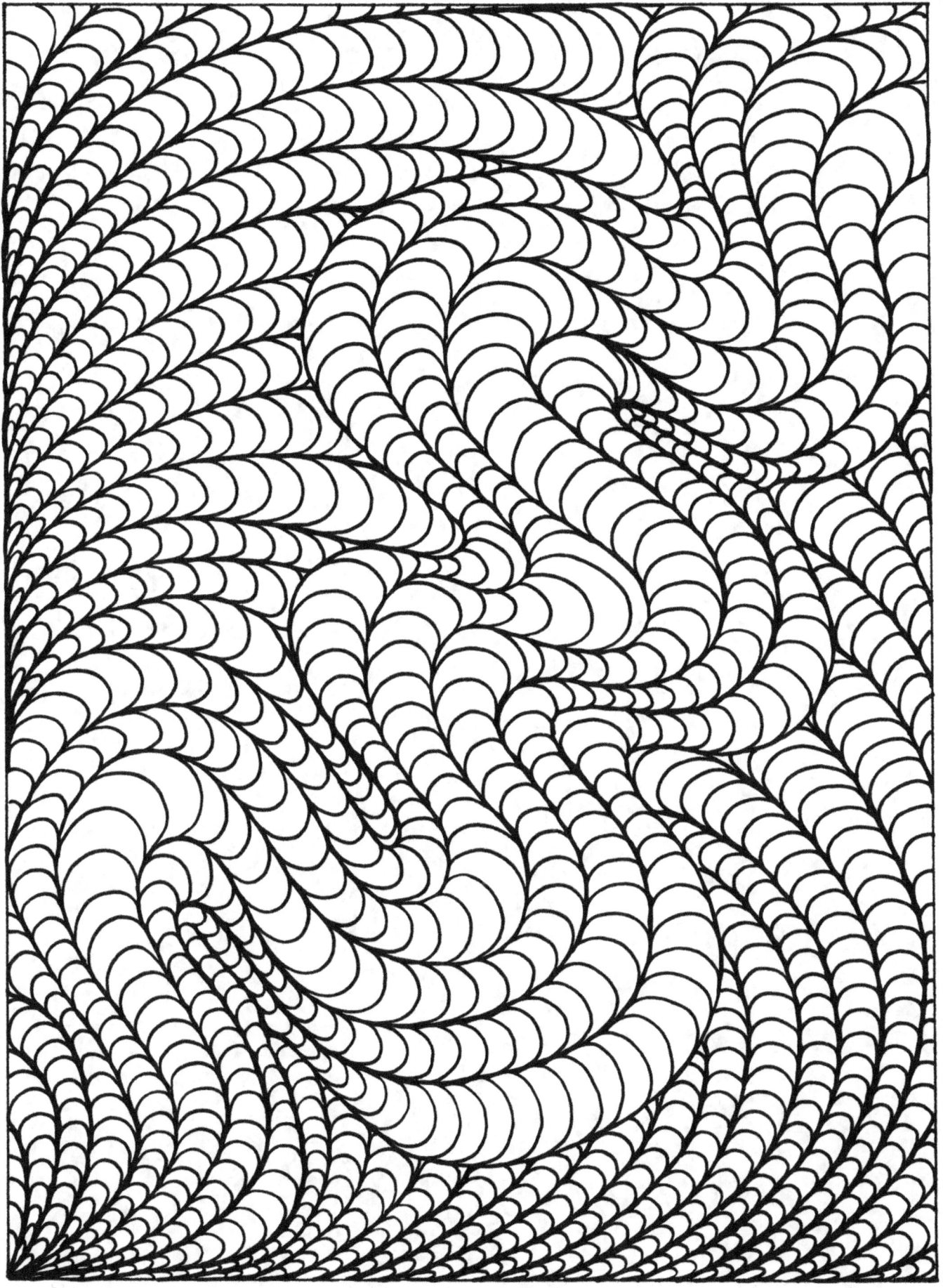

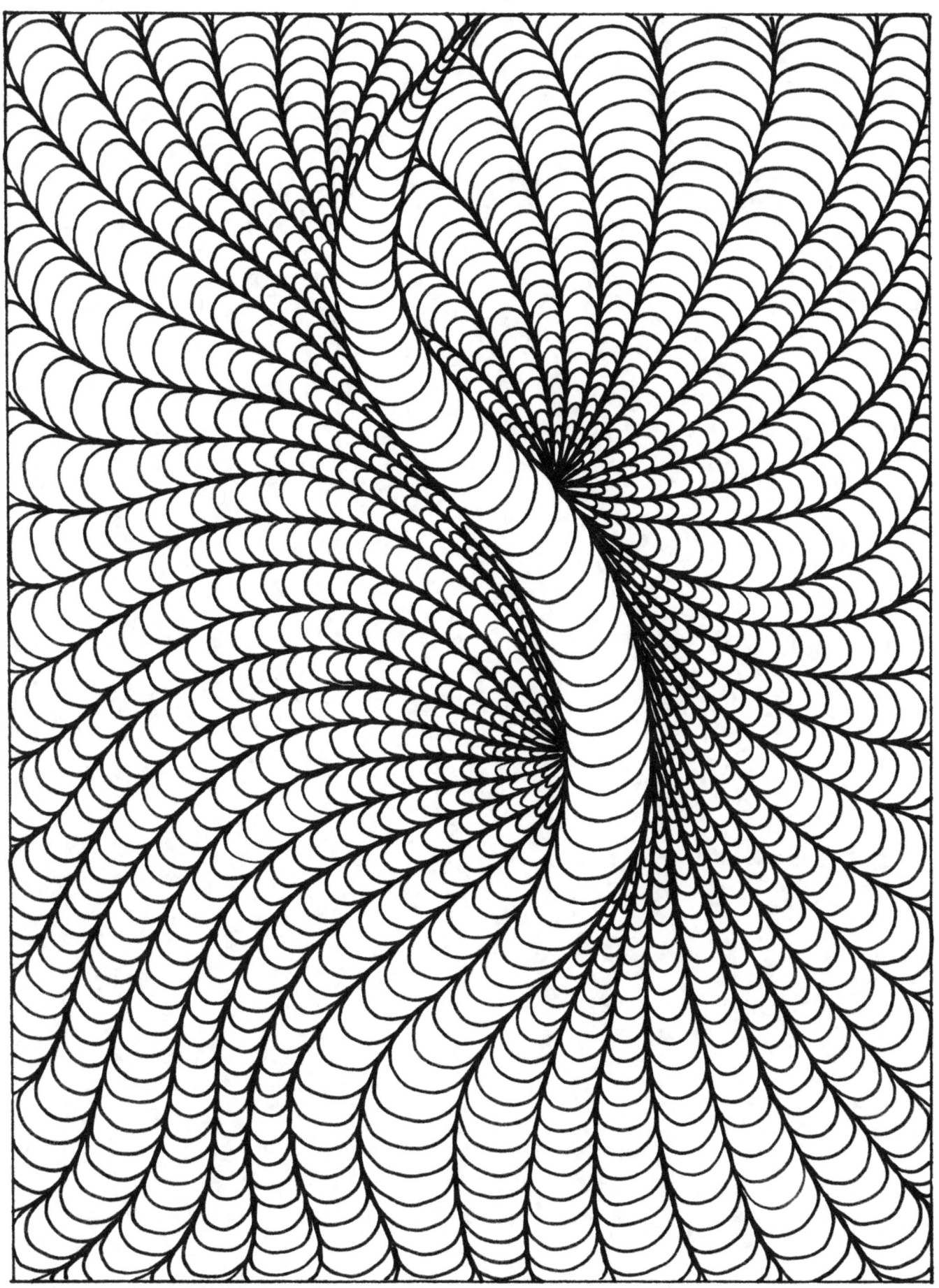

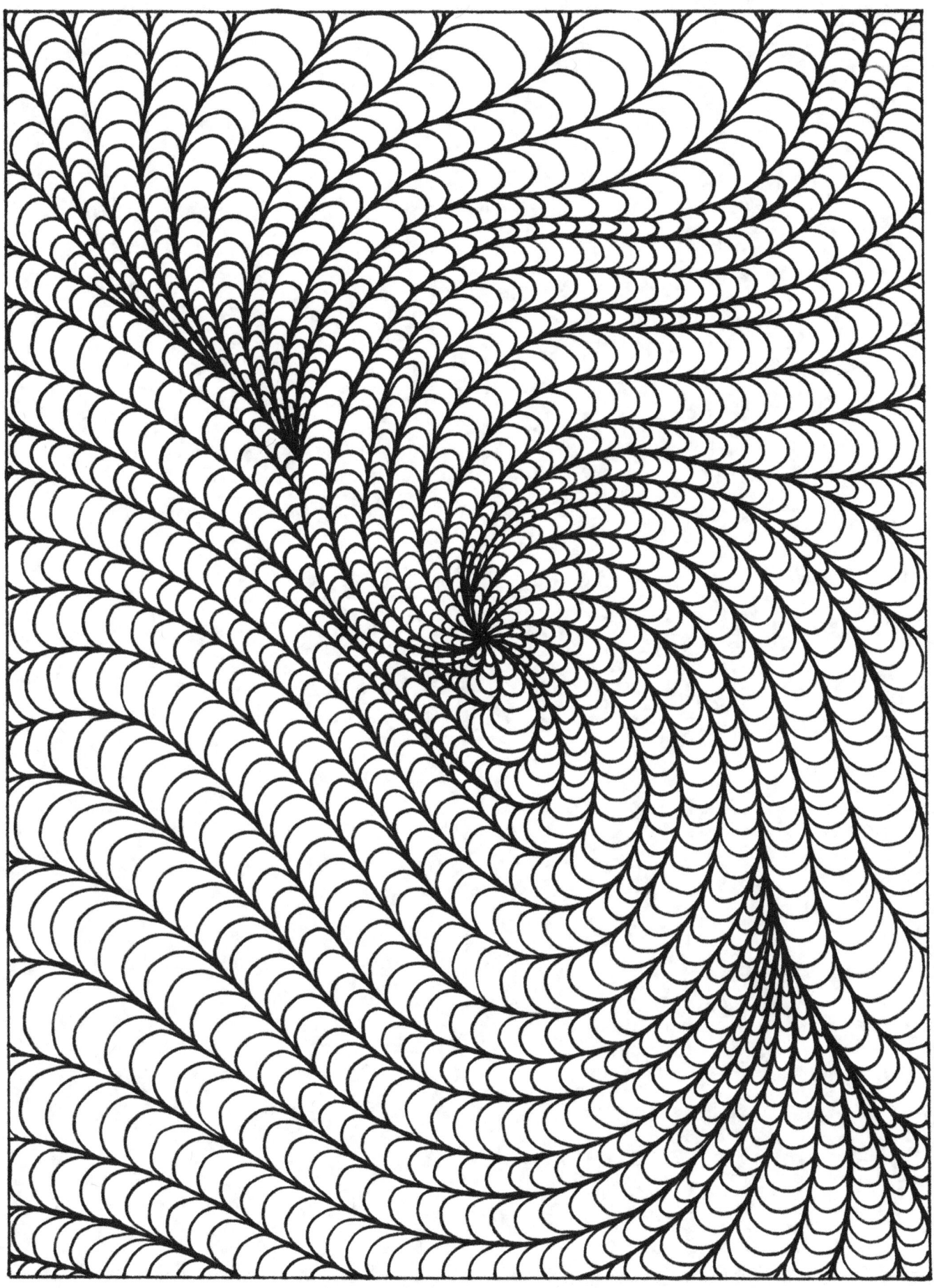

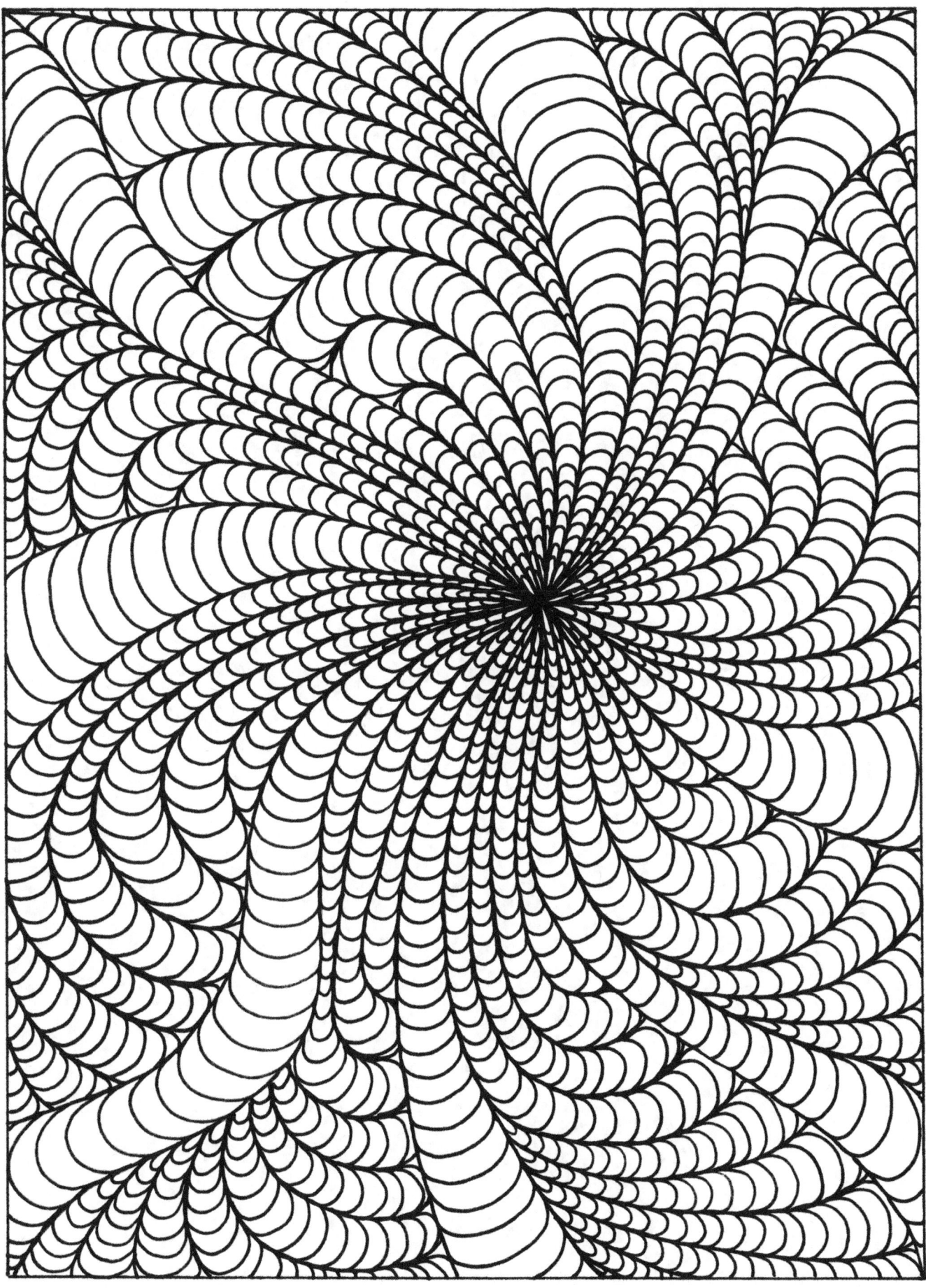

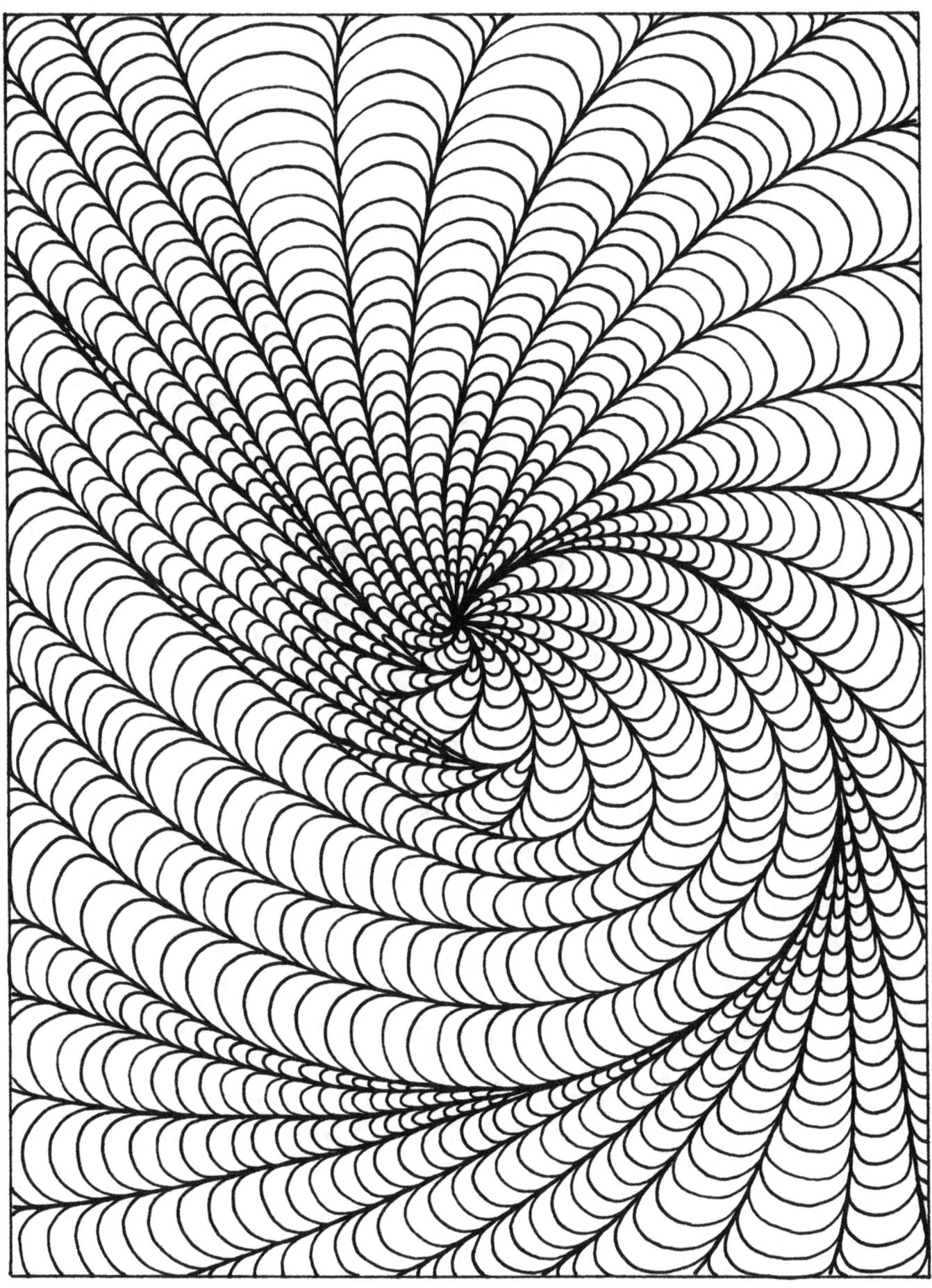

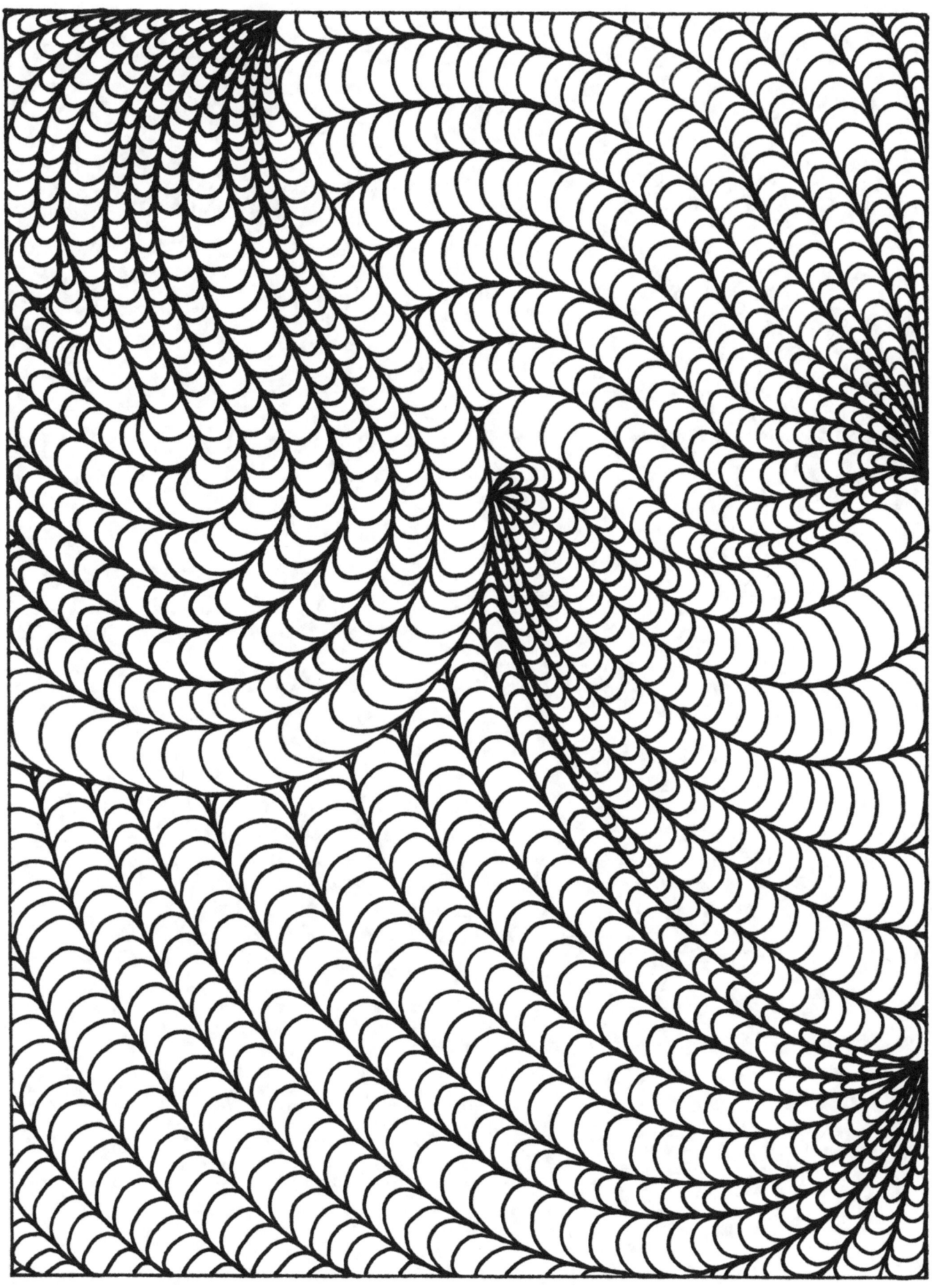

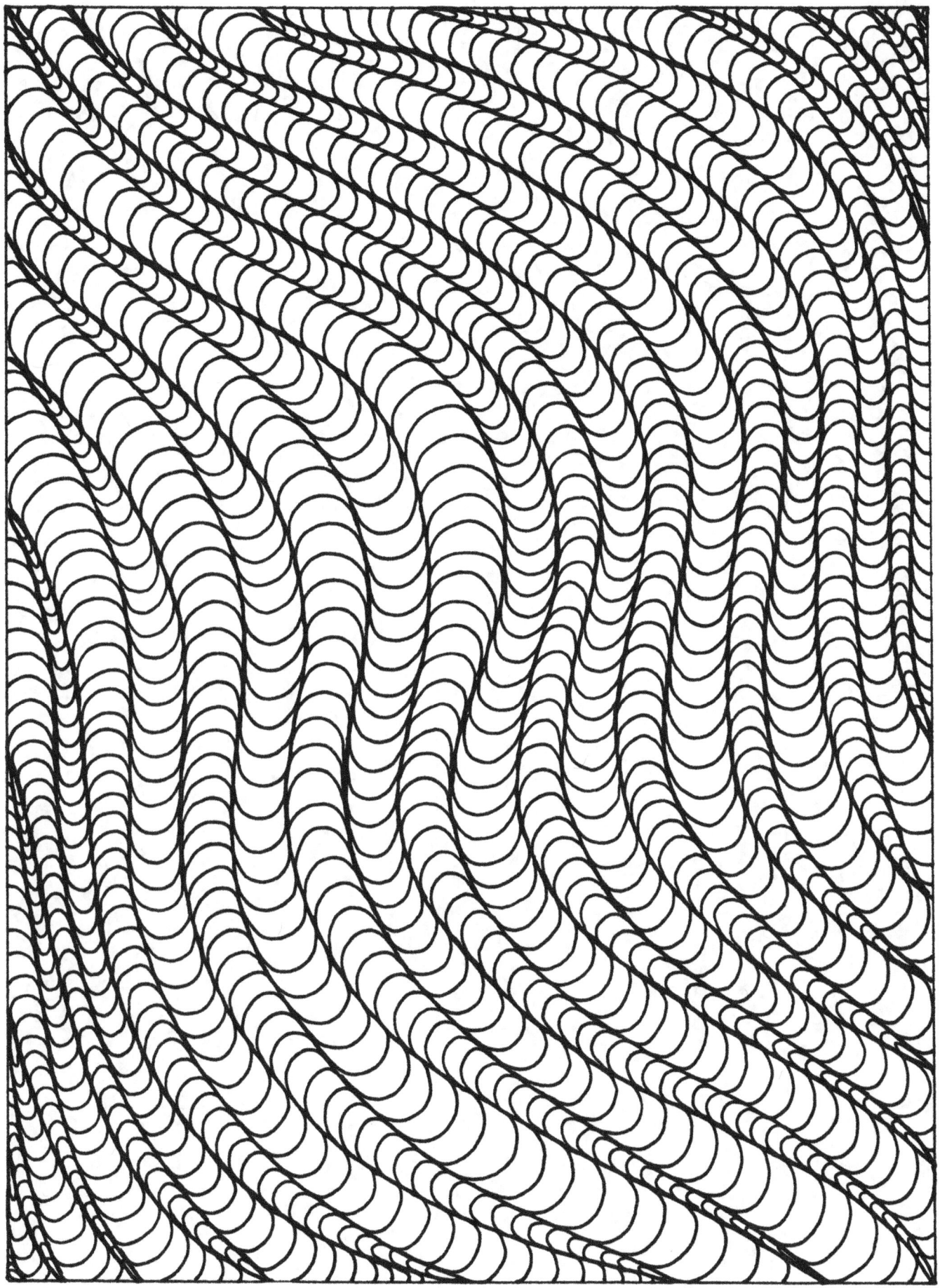

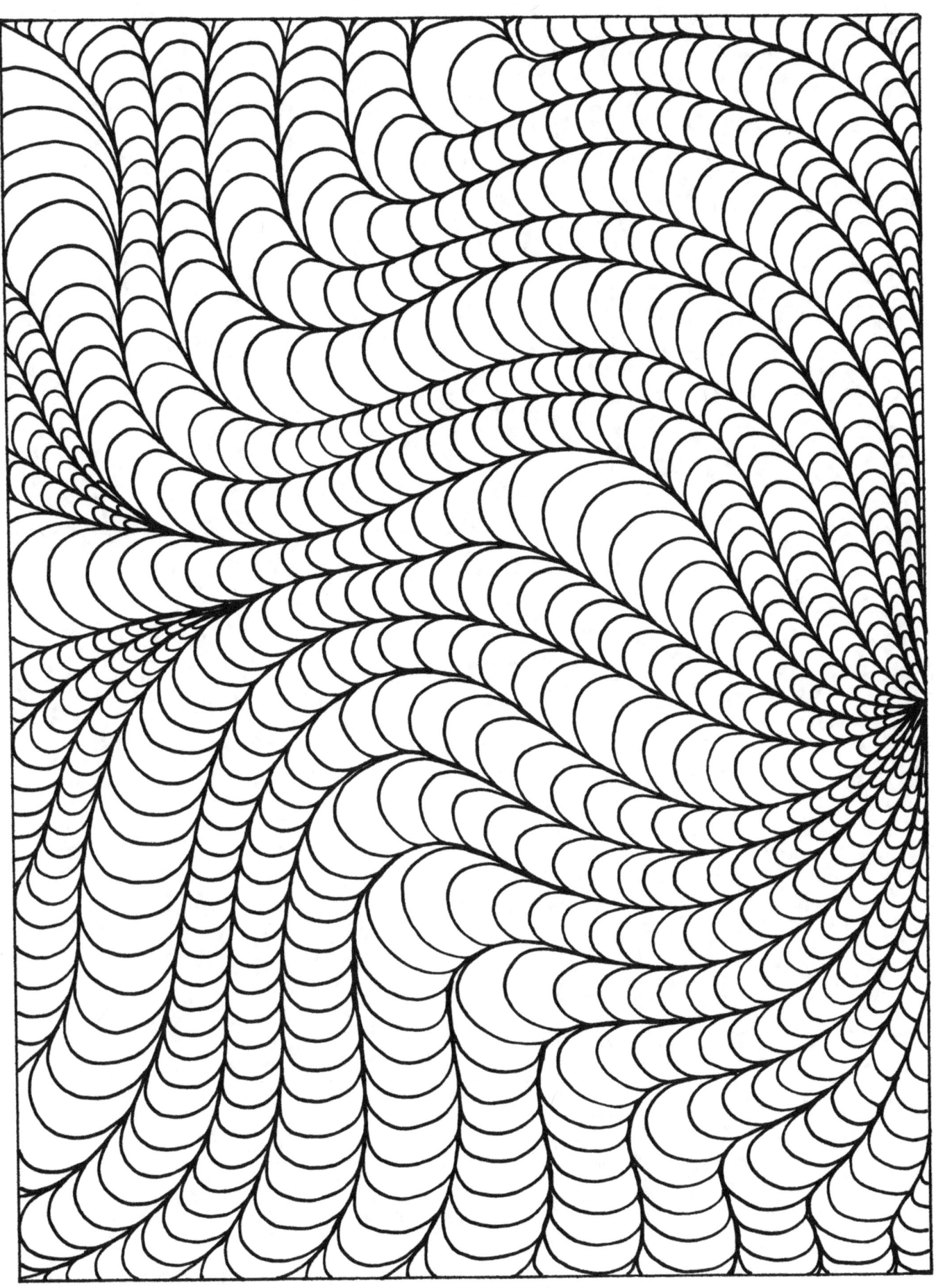

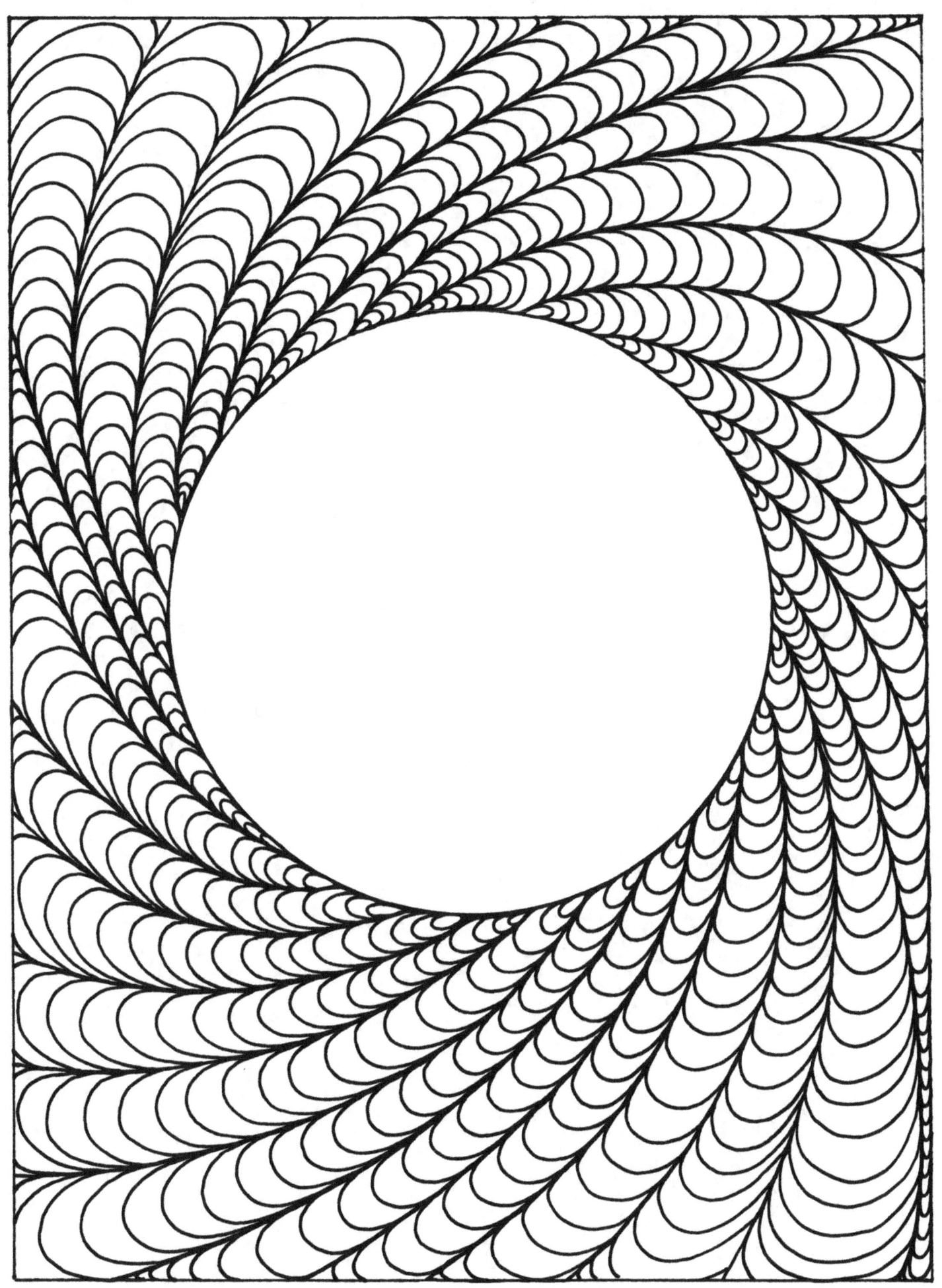

AMVW links etc

I hope you enjoyed my drawings, these are my personal destressers, I unwind and relax when I draw them, really my personal chill pill after long days of stress.....
-Anna-Marie V. Wedel

I would really appreciate that you mention my name when sharing...I love seeing your colored versions of my drawings ! Here are a few of my links if you want to see more of my art or throw my art page a like
Artpage: www.facebook.com/AMVWART
Color Pages of AMVW/ART: www.facebook.com/groups/ColorPagesOfAMVW/
and this is my tiny Payhip shop for huge color pages :
https://payhip.com/amvwart
Finally I am also the founder of "Global Doodle Gems" that you can find here:
www.facebook.com/groups/globaldoodlegems/
ohhh and the "Global Doodle Gems" official book page here: www.facebook.com/globaldoodlegems
My redbubble shop
http://www.redbubble.com/people/mariawedel
My society 6 shop
http://society6.com/amvwart
My Artmoney shop
http://www.artmoney.org/users/maria-wedel
YouTube channel
www.youtube.com/amvwart
Amazon profile
http://www.amazon.com/Global-Doodle-Gems/e/B0118G87NQ/ref=ntt_dp_epwbk_0

www.ingramcontent.com/pod-product-compliance
Lightning Source LLC
Chambersburg PA
CBHW082211220526
45470CB00010B/3120